WHERE
TWO *OR* THREE
ARE GATHERED

— WHERE —
TWO *OR* THREE
ARE GATHERED

ESSAYS ON FRIENDSHIP

EDITED BY SCOTT KEITH

Where Two or Three Are Gathered: Essays on Friendship

Scripture quotations marked (ESV) are from The ESV® Bible (The Holy Bible, English Standard Version®), copyright © 2001 by Crossway, a publishing ministry of Good News Publishers. Used by permission. All rights reserved.

Scripture quotations marked (NIV) are taken from the Holy Bible, New International Version®, NIV®. Copyright © 1973, 1978, 1984, 2011 by Biblica, Inc.™ Used by permission of Zondervan. All rights reserved worldwide. www .zondervan.com The "NIV" and "New International Version" are trademarks registered in the United States Patent and Trademark Office by Biblica, Inc.™

Scripture quotations marked (NKJV) taken from the New King James Version®. Copyright © 1982 by Thomas Nelson. Used by permission. All rights reserved.

Published by:
1517 Publishing
PO Box 54032
Irvine, CA 92619-4032

Publisher's Cataloging-In-Publication Data
(Prepared by The Donohue Group, Inc.)

Names: Keith, Scott Leonard, editor.
Title: Where two or three are gathered : essays on friendship / edited by Scott Keith.
Description: Irvine, CA : 1517 Publishing, [2019] | Includes bibliographical references.
Identifiers: ISBN 9781945500640 (hardcover) | ISBN 9781948969024 (softcover) | ISBN 9781948969031 (ebook)
Subjects: LCSH: Friendship—Religious aspects—Christianity. | Friendship—Philosophy. | Lutheran Church—Doctrines. | LCGFT: Essays.
Classification: LCC BV4647.F7 W44 2019 (print) | LCC BV4647.F7 (ebook) | DDC 241/.6762—dc23

Printed in the United States of America

Cover art by Brenton Clark Little

Contents

List of Abbreviations vii

Where Two or Three Are Gathered—An Introduction 1
  Scott L. Keith, PhD

Theology of Friendship 10
  Paul Koch, MDiv

Friendship in the Old Testament 17
  Chad Bird, MDiv, STM

Friendship in the New Testament 25
  Caleb E. Keith

The Invisible Bond of Friendship from Gilgamesh
    to Augustine 31
  Daniel van Voorhis, PhD

The Philosophy of Friendship 38
  Daniel Deen, PhD

The Ethics of Friendship 49
  Jeffrey C. Mallinson, DPhil

Luther and Melanchthon: A Reformation Friendship 68
  Scott L. Keith, PhD, and Caleb E. Keith

The Inklings: Friendship and Writing 75
  Samuel P. Schuldheisz, MDiv

Friendship and the Apologetics of Imagination:
  Middle-earth and Narnia 87
  Samuel P. Schuldheisz, MDiv

Friendship in the Lutheran Confessions: The Mutual
  Consolation of the Brethren. 97
  David J. Rufner, MDiv

Notes 107

Abbreviations

AE Luther, Martin. *Luther's Works,* American Edition. 55 vols. Edited by Jaroslav Pelikan and Helmut T. Lehman. Philadelphia: Muehlenberg and Fortress, and St. Louis: Concordia, 1955–86.

WA Luther, D. Martin. *Martin Luthers Werke. Kritische Gesamtausgabe.* 73 vols. Weimar: Herman Böhlaus, 1883–2009.

WATR Luther, D. Martin. *Martin Luthers Werke. Tischreden.* 6 vols. Weimar: Herman Böhlaus, 1912–21.

Trgl Bente, 1858–1930 F. *Concordia Triglotta. Triglot Concordia: The Symbolic Books of the Evangelical Lutheran Church, German, Latin, English. Published as a Memorial of the Quadricentenary Jubilee of the Reformation Anno Domini 1917 by Resolution of the Evangelical Lutheran Synod of Missouri, Ohio and Other States.* 1917.

BOC Kolb, Robert, Timothy J. Wengert, and Charles P. Arand. *The Book of Concord: The Confessions of the Evangelical Lutheran Church.* Minneapolis: Fortress Press, 2000.

SC *Luther's Small Catechism and Explanation.* Concordia Publishing House. 1991.

CR Melanchthon, Philipp. *Corpus Reformatorum: Ph. Melanchtonis opera quae supersunt Omnia. 28 vols. Halis Saxonum: C.S. Schwetschke, 1834–60.*

Where Two or Three Are Gathered— An Introduction

Scott L. Keith, PhD

> Throughout life, a faithful friend is a very great blessing and a very precious treasure.
>
> —Martin Luther

The Sound of Friendship

Not too long ago, I went back to the small town where my wife and I lived while we were raising our children. We lived in Carson City, Nevada, and spent our time between there and my mother's home in nearby Gardnerville. In those days, I worked for the city, managing the youth programs within the recreation department. (All *Parks and Rec* jokes will now be accepted.) There were two other people in my office. One was a young woman, who worked alongside me. The other was a man named Joel, who ran the sports programs. We all became excellent lifelong friends. To this day, I would do anything for them, and I believe they'd say the same of me.

I decided to connect with Joel on our last visit. He was on his way to take a trailer load of trash to the dump when I called. He said, "Are you at your mom's?"

I answered, "Yes."

He said, "I'll be there in ten minutes."

We spent the remainder of the day together, riding around in his truck, going to the dump, getting lunch, and talking. We talked as if no time at all had passed. We picked up as though we still worked in that same little office together.

Our conversations were not too complicated. In other words, we did not try to solve all of the problems in the world. We just talked about our lives, our children, our trucks, and current endeavors. We were once more walking side-by-side as friends. In a small way, it was rather glorious. Even though it didn't sound like anything other than two guys hanging out, it was still, nonetheless, glorious.

This is what friendship between men often sounds and looks like.

Service Is Vocation

I think that having at least a few good friends is a good work of sorts. I say this because a friendship is a relationship where the people of God have opportunities to serve one another regularly, and even irregularly.

This might seem counterintuitive. After all, we often see good works as pious acts or sacrificial deeds. Most good works, however, look rather common whether they are done in or outside of the church. Time after time, good works are more common and take the shape of ordinary people, in common relationships, doing everyday things.

Even though friendship is one of the most common relationships of life—often first formed when we are still small children—when they grow and mature, they become much more than playdates and hanging out. Friendship becomes one of the ways where two or three gather together in Jesus' name, and when they do so, Jesus comes and dwells in their midst.

Life gains meaning when we as Christians serve one another as little Christs in the world. We serve God by freely helping one another in love. Good friendships provide one of the mechanisms through which God calls people into our lives whom we can serve, often by merely being present for them as friends. These friendships where we freely serve and are freely served are great gifts from God even though they might go overlooked. So, as C.S. Lewis once claimed, while good friendships are not necessary for life, they are essential and give meaning to life.

This Is a Dangerous Idea

There are many examples of friends serving one another in life. Some are extreme and extravagant, but most are ordinary. I've heard many stories that have inspired me to look for good friends with whom I can engage and be engaged. I am a writer and teacher, so one of the friendship stories I've gravitated to the most is that of the Inklings of Oxford University.

The Inklings were an informal literary circle in Oxford that began meeting in the early 1930s and continued until the late 1940s. The core of the group consisted of C.S. Lewis and J.R.R. Tolkien. The group took particular pleasure in listening to one another read their works, which were in progress, aloud. Lewis and Tolkien invited other well-known and not-so-well-known authors to join them for informal, convivial meetings in Oxford pubs, later adding evening gatherings to read their works aloud, after which they would receive both praise and honest criticism. Gradually, the schedule of the Inklings' meetings became regularized, so they generally met on Tuesday mornings at the Eagle and Child pub (which they called the "Bird and Baby" or just the "Bird") and at Lewis's study rooms at Magdalen College at the University of Oxford on Thursday evenings. At the pub, they smoked their pipes, drank, and enjoyed good food (almost like hobbits). While they sat in the bar, they talked about language and literature.

As I've heard it described by those in the know, the Inklings were not afraid to mix it up a bit. These men were not all alike. Lewis was brash and boisterous. Tolkien seems to have been more reserved and introspective. (Not unlike Martin Luther and Philip Melanchthon, as you will read in a later chapter.) They did not agree on many things. Tolkien is said to have believed that Lewis's use of allegory in his *Space Trilogy* and *Chronicles of Narnia* lacked the subtlety fitting an Oxford don. Even more personally, they often disagreed on moral and social issues.

Despite their differences, they still met. They took the time to assemble because friendship, creativity, and debate are essential. They acknowledged that friendship, especially male friendship, does not work when focused on the other friend. Friends, as Lewis says in *The Four Loves,* walk alongside each other and cast their gaze together at something else, something outside themselves. In our current cultural milieu, this is a dangerous idea. When we cast our gaze on something else, some other topic, some other work, or some different concept, we open ourselves to the possibility of disagreement. Conversations between real friends are dangerous in that while friends walk alongside one another, their time is sometimes spent in a heated debate about the object of their discussion.

We need to regain some of these dangerous friendships. We need friendships like what Lewis and Tolkien shared—a friendship of this kind, defined by two people (at least two people) taking the initiative and making the time to share, care, and listen to the ideas of the other. This listening will then turn into an examination and critique of the ideas proposed. Review and analysis will in due time result in a debate over the ideas. The debate is where the danger arises, but it is also where we experience iron sharpening iron. And as "Iron sharpens iron," the Proverb says, "one man sharpens another."

To accomplish this, we need friends who are not like us, at least not wholly like us. To be a midwife to an idea or a work for another, the concept and work cannot be what we would have produced ourselves. Recent data suggests that our brains grow when paired in a creative enterprise with another person. When we converse and create together, we become better.

The Inklings were useful as a group because of their intellectual and personality differences. As Lewis explains in *An Experiment in Criticism*, there is not one person among us who holds all of the great ideas. So the creative process demands that we develop friendships with people who are not like and do not think exactly like us, and that we hunger for rational opposition.

Lewis scholar Diana Glyer began a paper I heard recently by saying, "If you want to be like Lewis, you need a little more Tolkien in your life."[1] Though the two men were friends, they did have a falling out of sorts in the late 1940s. To my way of thinking, this only shows that they were both sinners, not that they were not friends. The proof of their enduring mutual friendship and respect comes late. In 1961, long after the Inklings disbanded, Lewis nominated Tolkien for the Nobel Prize in Literature for his benchmark work, *The Lord of the Rings*. Tolkien did not win the prize, but Lewis's nomination of his friend shows that he never lost respect for him or his sense of intellectual hospitality.

I want to be more like Lewis. Therefore, I need a little more Tolkien in my life. That is why I have, for as long as I can remember now, attempted to invite men into my life who are different than me. I need a Tolkien to my Lewis (if only). Danger is good. And when two or three gather, they have the freedom to challenge and serve one another at the same time.

A Necessary Topic for Today

I have spent a few pages explaining some reasons why I think we all, but especially men, need at least a few good friends.[2] If I am correct, then why do more than 10 million American men say they have no close friends? Why has male loneliness been named as a public health crisis? Maybe because we have devalued the idea of friendship. We have certainly devalued the need for men to gather together in true friendship.

When surveyed, just over half (61 percent) of men say they have two or fewer friends. In the United States, that approximates to around 75 million men! Furthermore, one in eight men overall said they have no friends. The data from these surveys suggest that men tend to have fewer close friends as they get older. Only 7 percent of those under twenty-four say they have no friends with whom they would discuss a serious topic, but 19 percent of those over fifty-five say the same.[3] Surprisingly (perhaps), married men are one-third more likely than their single counterparts to say they have no one to turn to outside of the home. What this means is that millions of men are experiencing a sense of profound loss that haunts them even though they are engaged in fully realized romantic relationships, marriages, and families.

Men report that they feel as though society has unrealistic expectations of them. They also report that they are expected to be all things to those in their lives yet do so without making real connections with other men outside of the home. They are supposed to be happy being isolated to the house and the responsibilities that lie therein. They are expected to act like they don't need other men. Men are supposed to spend time with their wives. That's normal, natural, and very healthy, but it often comes with the cost of declining friendships. Their marriage is rated as essential; their friendships are estimated as luxuries. This attitude needs to change.

As a result, more than 6 million American men report that they are depressed.[4] Grown men have a suicide rate three times that of women.[5] Men don't share and say they are less comfortable striking up new friendships, increasing this sense of isolation and loneliness. Men tend to engage in a constant risk versus reward analysis. Risk: my wife will be pissed off, or I'll miss another one of my kid's soccer games if I spend needed time with my friends. Reward: I'll have time with my friends. Wife and children usually win out (as they should) over time with a friend or friends.

This mentality has not always been the case. Once men would gather together in lodges, fraternal organizations, or social groups. These are now disappearing or have completely disappeared. Dad used to golf on the weekend and got to the lodge on Wednesday night. Not now! Now he plays a taxi driver. As the earlier data illustrated, maybe some of this time would be better spent among friends. Men need friends!

I have collected the essays in this book to explore the now-countercultural idea of friendship, specifically male friendship, and why we all need at least a few good friends. We will explore male friendship as a gift from God and why friendship is a means by which we do good by being little Christs to each other, especially as we encourage and forgive one another in the name of Christ. As a side benefit to the presence of Christ among them, when two or three gather, loneliness and the resulting depression mentioned above are often reduced considerably.

Making It Important

A few years ago, my good friend Dave planned a backpacking trip to go to the Escalante National Wilderness on a sixty-mile, six-day hike. He invited three other men, making our expedition party a total of five. The first day's hike was grueling. We intended to make ten miles, but as soon as we set out to hike, we ended up clawing and climbing only three. This did not make for a good start. The next day was no better; in fact, it was worse. We climbed sheer cliffs, dodged poison ivy, and plodded just another five miles. We were two days in and twelve miles behind schedule. Our attitudes sucked. We wanted to kill Dave (kind of but not really), and we needed to change the plan.

So, we planned to cut twelve miles from the overall route and continue on this rigorous hike—which we all now call our death march—through the Utah wilderness. Our trip did not get any better. We had planned to drink and talk into the wee hours of the morning every night after our hike. In reality, we were all so exhausted at the end of every day that we just climbed into our sleeping bags and fell asleep as soon as our heads hit the rocks we used as pillows.

But an odd thing happened on day three. We all stopped threatening to kill Dave, and we bonded together to get to the end. We talked to pass the time and get our minds off the blisters. We sang songs. We got to know one another better (even those who were new to the group). We farted and joked. We warned one another of peril and locked arms to ford rivers. We became friends. We became brothers.

This reminiscing is not meant to imply that we all hold a great sense of nostalgia for the trip. I still call it a death march. But we are all the better for having finished together. The most significant thing that happened as a result of the trip, however, is the letter I received from my friend Dave about a month after we all returned home.

Dave sent me a handwritten note explaining why he felt the trip was necessary in the first place and apologizing for his unintentional ignorance regarding the difficulty of the task he had set before us. He asked for my forgiveness. At the time, I assumed he already knew we were "all good." But what he needed was absolution. He needed to hear the words. He needed his friend to tell him that no grudges remained between us. He still needed our friendship. If my memory serves me correctly, I called him (maybe texted) and said to him that in the name of Jesus, I forgave him.

Dave is a remarkable man. Don't get me wrong; he is a sinner and too ambitious of a trip planner. But for his whole life, Dave has intentionally sought out friends in a way that was foreign to me until some years ago. He too knew, in a down-to-earth sort of way, what sometimes escapes me—that real friendship is about mutual consolation and forgiveness. This is how we freely serve the neighbors who we call friends.

Mutual Consolation of the Brethren

Martin Luther once claimed:

> Having a friend is a great blessing . . . This is true not only in the common dangerous difficulties of normal life wherein they may offer help and consolation but also in spiritual matters. For even though the heart is led to faith by the Holy Spirit, there is nonetheless a great advantage in having a friend with whom you can talk about religion and the Gospel, and from whom you may hear the words of absolution and forgiveness.[6]

Friendship is about forgiveness. Luther, I think, understood this fact better than most. He was not the easiest of men to be around. By his own admission, he was a rough, boisterous, and difficult person. While he corresponded with countless people on matters personal and spiritual, he only had a few close friends. But despite his temperamental nature—or perhaps because of it—Luther knew friends are given to us by God to forgive us.

My friend Dave will have more to say about this in a later chapter. For now, it is enough to say that you will notice a theme in this book. That theme is the mutual consolation and conversation of the brethren (or the people of God). In the Smalcald Articles, Luther says:

> We will now return to the Gospel, which not merely in one way gives us counsel and aid against sin; for God is superabundantly rich in His grace. First, through the spoken Word by which the forgiveness of sins is preached in the whole world; which is the peculiar office of the Gospel. Secondly, through Baptism. Thirdly, through the holy Sacrament of the Altar. Fourthly, through the power of the keys, and also through the mutual conversation and consolation of brethren, Matt. 18:20: Where two or three are gathered together, etc.[7]

In other words, friends are given for multiple reasons: to be there in times of joy and need, to serve one another, to provide a sounding board and give advice, to challenge, and most of all to speak to one another the words of Christ—I forgive you.

The Plan

The plan for this book is somewhat simple. I have collected essays from many of my friends. They will speak to you about the theology and philosophy of friendship. Friendships in the Old and New Testament are explored, as well as friendships in history. You will even hear about the Inklings again. And in the end, my friend Dave will teach you about the idea of friendship in the Lutheran Confessions.

All of these chapters reflect the unique character of the authors. Some are academic, others are pastoral, while the rest are more down to earth. Not all of my friends are alike, and thus not all of the chapters in this little book are alike. Yet, there is something uniquely special about this work on friendship written by a group of friends. Several of us have been friends for over twenty-five years; others met no more than a few years ago. We are all friends and value teaching you a little more about what we hold so dear. I hope you enjoy this short work given to you by your friends at 1517.

Scott L. Keith, PhD
Easter, 2019

Theology of Friendship

Paul Koch, MDiv

There are many things for which we have and perhaps even need a theology. The classic *Loci* of the church provide a good sampling of theological treatises—the nature of God, the divinity of Christ, the means of grace, God's law and Gospel, creation, salvation, and sanctification, to name but a few. To speak about such things and have meaningful conversations with our friends and neighbors requires some measure of an understood theology. To speak about them with any sense of accuracy and authority, one must attend to what God says about them. So, to have a theology (at least a theology that strives to be faithful) is to be driven first to the Word of God, to the source of God's revelation of himself.

While we may find or perhaps even develop a theology for just about anything that catches our fancy, not all theologies will flow naturally from the Word of God. Even more, not everything we do requires a theology. While I may be able to create a delightful little theology of pipe smoking and bourbon drinking, it doesn't make it necessary or all that useful to my neighbor. No doubt, such a theology will give value and meaning to my evening ritual on the front porch, but such a theology would not flow freely from the Word. My pipe-smoking and bourbon-drinking theology would no doubt employ a certain amount of intellectual gymnastics. In the end, it would resemble a type of pointy-headed theological entertainment rather than contributing to any meaningful conversation. To go searching for a theology of things that don't need a theology is usually a sure-fire way to waste your time on the obscure and unimportant.

Which brings us to our precarious topic. My first reaction to the suggestion that I write a *theology of friendship* was one of suspicion. Friendship, it seems, is one of the things in this world that doesn't need a theology. Friendships certainly exist without a theology being articulated. They exist in equal strength both within the church and outside. I doubt believers in the Triune God have more and better-quality friendships than those who are Buddhist or Muslim. In fact, I am not convinced that having a theology of friendship will actually improve the friendships you have.

And yet, there is something about friendship that demands our attention. Friendship has the ability to defy the corrosive effects of time calamity, suffering, and even sin. In fact, these things can make it stronger. Perhaps if we could understand this force, even harness it, we might find a source of joy and strength that is unrivaled in the daily grind. Perhaps developing a theology of friendship will help us value the friendships that currently exist without a theology and impact those friends who are already walking beside us. Perhaps in an age saturated in social media "friends," a theology of friendship is just what we need.

Before doing so, we need to define our subject. So, just what is friendship? For what exactly should we search in the Scriptures? There is no institution of friendship by our God. There is no moment where this relationship is established by the Creator or boundaries for it, as compared to the relationship between a man and his wife or parents and their children. We even have foundations for a king and his subjects and a priest and the faithful, but there is no prescription for what makes one a friend or how to find a friend. Certainly our Lord speaks about being a friend, who his friends are, and what he does for them, but that is a long way from establishing the parameters of friendship itself. Where did this relationship come from? What is its source?

The answer may not be what we want to hear. We may be hoping for this great, benevolent gift of God establishing for you a friend to share your load, to build you up, or to keep your secrets. But that is not what we find. Rather, the beginning of friendship flows from a much more sinister font. C.S. Lewis's monumental work, *The Four Loves,* gets us started with this observation:

Every real Friendship is a sort of secession, even a rebellion. It may be a rebellion of serious thinkers against accepted clap-trap or of faddist against accepted good sense; of real artist against popular ugliness or of charlatans against civilized taste; of good men against the badness of society or of bad men against its goodness. Whichever it is, it will be unwelcomed to Top People. In each knot of Friends there is a sectional 'public opinion' which fortifies its members against the public opinion of the community in general. Each therefore is a pocket of potential resistance. Men who have real Friends are less easy to manage or 'get at'; harder for good Authorities to correct or for bad Authorities to corrupt.[1]

The origin of the force we know as friendship is not found in divine institution but in rebellion.

As we observe the development of a friendship, we see the rise of a subset within a larger group. There is a perimeter that is drawn within the larger population. By way of example, let's suppose that in a given high school, the senior class consists of one hundred students. These one hundred students will have common experiences, share classrooms, and wear the same cap and gowns on graduation day. But no doubt, within this group of one hundred, there are many smaller groups of three, four, five, or more individuals. They then form their own perimeter within the population of the senior class. There is a different sense of loyalty among these friends, a different value system, a different accountability system, and different goals. As Lewis said, these friend groups are "a pocket of potential resistance." Resistance to what? Resistance to the values and goals of the larger group.

Rebellion is a strange place to begin. It doesn't begin at creation; it begins at the fall. As Eve is tempted by the serpent, she begins to doubt the Word of God. Will she die or not? Can it really be as bad as all that? She desires to exercise her will independent of her Creator, to become like God, knowing good and evil. In the end, she doesn't do this alone. She needs a friend. She needs one who would join her in a newly established perimeter within the created order. "When the woman saw that the tree was good for food, and that it was a delight to the eyes, and that the tree was to be desired to make one wise, she took of its fruit and ate, and she also gave some to her husband *who was with her*, and he ate" (Gen. 3:6 ESV; emphasis added).

It makes sense, then, that as God enters the garden, his first words are, "Where are you?" Not that the omniscient God didn't know their location but rather that his creatures had pulled away and hidden themselves. His words act as a confession of a new reality, where they will head out on their own in rebellion, in opposition to their God. Humankind would now form friendships in their sin and so make their stand upon the earth.

A good example follows in the story of the Tower of Babel. Here we might say that friendship is found in a common tongue, along with a desire to bind together and not be forgotten in time. They say, "Come, let us build ourselves a city and a tower with its top in the heavens, and let us make a name for ourselves, lest we be dispersed over the face of the whole earth" (Gen. 11:4 ESV). What better image of a perimeter within the created population. These people actually begin to build with brick and mortar, to construct a physical protection for their rebellion. Looking down, God sees their strength and their resolve, and he says, "Behold they are one people, and they have all one language, and this is only the beginning of what they will do. And nothing that they propose to do will now be impossible for them" (Gen. 11:6 ESV). Here is a testimony to the powerful force that is friendship. What they desire to do, they will do. They will make their own values, construct their own goals, and create their own languages. So, God squashes the rebellion by confusing their language, and once again they are dispersed over the face of all the earth.

Nevertheless, over time new friendships would be formed. New rebellions would rise up as humankind tried to make their stand and control their own destiny. Some would have success for a time. Some would be brutal and harsh, and some would even seek to rule over others. Friendships would grow to become tribes and nations where new rebellions formed. But in the end, they would all fail. Every rebellion, every friendship would collapse on itself until something unpredictable—that surpassed all human understanding—happened. The rebellion of friendship would forever fail until God himself joined in.

The promise of Immanuel (God with us) is the promise of something more for friendship. We are told that "when the fullness of time had come, God sent forth his Son, born of woman, born under the law, to redeem those who were under the law, so that we might receive adoption as sons" (Gal. 4:4–5 ESV). The Son of God enters into his own creation to take up the cause of sinners who forever failed in their rebellion against God. He lives, loves, and weeps with the rebellion. He is "one who in every respect has been tempted as we are, yet without sin" (Heb. 4:15 ESV).

As our Lord speaks about his reception into the rebellion, about what people within the perimeter have to say about him, he says this:

> But to what shall I compare this generation? It is like children sitting in the marketplaces and calling to their playmates, "We played the flute for you, and you did not dance; we sang a dirge, and you did not mourn." For John [the Baptist] came neither eating nor drinking, and they say, "He has a demon." The Son of Man came eating and drinking, and they say, "Look at him! A glutton and a drunkard, *a friend of tax collectors and sinners!*" Yet wisdom is justified by her deeds. (Matt. 11:16–19 ESV; emphasis added)

The interesting thing is that Jesus doesn't deny this title. He doesn't reject being called a friend of sinners. If anything, Scripture seems to double down on this notion. When the Pharisees accuse our Lord of hanging out with sinners, after the calling of Levi the tax collector to be his disciple, he answers, "Those who are well have no need of a physician, but those who are sick. I came not to call the righteous, but sinners" (Mark 2:17 ESV). Our Lord makes friends with sinners; he joins them by being one of them. As Isaiah said, "[He] was numbered with the transgressors" (Isa. 53:12). In fact, according to St. Paul, not only does Jesus become friends with sinners but he embraces the depth of their rebellion as his own, for this is how he would reconcile the rebellion to God. He says, "For our sake he made him to be sin who knew no sin, so that in him we might become the righteousness of God" (2 Cor. 5:21).

And so, Jesus says to his disciples, "Greater love has no one than this, that someone lay down his life for his friends. You are my friends if you do what I command you. No longer do I call you servants, for the servant does not know what his master is doing; but I have called you friends, for all that I have heard from my Father I have made known to you" (John 15:13–15). He knows that joining this rebellion will cost him his life. Yet, because he laid down his life for his friends, love would win the day, for the love of this friend changes everything. It brings hope and reconciliation and the promise of something new. Friendship itself changes by this one who chooses to be friends with sinners, this one who chooses to join in the rebellion, and this one who chooses to die so that he might provide a way to victory.

Jesus is the fulfillment of the greatest longing of friendship. In this friend of sinners, we find more than a passing shadow of friendship but something sure and solid. In our Lord we are given the perfection of friendship. Some fifty years before our Lord was born, the great Roman orator Cicero examined the longing for and nature of true friendship. Despite his unbelief in the almighty God, even he could recognize the incomprehensible power of a true friend. He wrote,

> Great and numerous as are the blessing of friendship, this certainly is the sovereign one, that it gives us bright hopes for the future and forbids weakness and despair. In the face of a true friend a man sees as it were a second self. So that where his friend is he is; if his friend be rich, he is not poor; though he be weak, his friend's strength is his; and in his friend's life he enjoys a second life after his own is finished.[2]

The Word of God became flesh, dwelt among us, and became our friend. That friend suffered and died for the rebellion; he died as one of us. But the Word did not stay dead; the Word that did its work in the flesh of a friend rose from the grave. We have gone from rebellion to reconciliation, from enemies to friends. We can sing joyfully, "What a Friend we have in Jesus," and all go merrily on our way. This is not the end, though; there is still a rebellion. There is still a perimeter within the population. The tables have turned, however, for in the life of our Friend, we have been given a second life.

That Word continues to work right now, as he proclaims life, hope, and forgiveness. The powerful force that we know of as friendship is now a tool used for his work. The rebellion is now made up of brothers and sisters in Christ who have drawn a perimeter within the rebellion of the world. Being reconciled to God through the life, death, and resurrection of the Friend who chose us establishes a new order and a new reality.

By the power of that external Word, we now speak rebellion into the ears of our brothers and sisters. We speak of death to the arrogant, proud, and self-righteous. We speak life and promise to the brokenhearted, to the fearful and doubting, and to the wounded and emptyhanded. Here, in the Word of Christ, our friendships begin anew. Here, they are transformed into something powerful, something that resists the deteriorating sands of time, something that holds echoes of eternity itself. For friendship bound up in the external Word of God becomes a formidable tool of the Gospel.

Luther seemed to be driving this point home when he wrote in the Smalcald Articles,

> We now want to return to the gospel, which gives guidance and help against sin in more than one way, because God is extravagantly rich in his grace: first, through the spoken word, in which the forgiveness of sins is preached to the whole world (which is the proper function of the gospel); second, through baptism; third, through the holy Sacrament of the Altar; four, through the power of the keys and also through the mutual conversation and consolation of brothers and sisters. Matthew 18:20: "Where two or three are gathered . . ."[3]

The *mutual conversation and consolation of brothers and sisters* is how the rebellion of the Gospel continues to endure in a world bound by sin, death, and the devil. Friendship may not need a theology. It does not need explanation and dissection to be a powerful force in our lives, and certainly friendships do not need the church to be good friendships or, for that matter, lasting friendships. However, I don't think the reverse can be so confidently said. I don't know that the church can last for very long without friendship. Just as the original rebellion required men who stand side by side to draw their perimeter, so today those who are gathered by the gifts of Christ must gather together. We will need others who will bear the external Word for us. In so doing, we will make our stand against the Devil, the world, and our own sinful hearts.

The handing over of the goods—that is, the proclamation of salvation by grace through faith in Christ alone—will continually call for the creation and endurance of friendship. By friendship we will keep the perimeter until our Lord, the Friend of Sinners, returns.

Friendship in the Old Testament

Chad Bird, MDiv, STM

I for my part consider the loss of all my possessions less important than that of a faithful friend.

—Martin Luther

In the small classroom nestled in the heart of the small campus was a room big on blackboards. Two full walls were blanketed by them. And by the time our sixty minutes was up, hardly a square inch remained free of chalk. Latin declensions and Greek paradigms, written in a masterful hand, danced across the room.

Our professor, Richard Dinda, guided me and my university friends for three years through the labyrinth of these languages. One year in Latin, two in Greek. He opened our eyes to the riches awaiting us in the original languages of the *Aeneid*, the New Testament, and the early church fathers. By the time he was finished with us, we possessed the linguistic tools we needed for a lifetime of study, reflection, writing, and research.

But we had something else as well, something unexpected: a deeper and broader understand of the world, as well as ourselves. We hadn't anticipated this when we signed up for his courses. It wasn't on the syllabus. We certainly didn't imagine our tuition was paying for it. But there it was—an unexpected gift.

On a weekly basis, as we wrestled with texts, our professor would open up a new vista for us. It was like exploring an abandoned house, room by room, still full of the former occupant's possessions. In a slow and steady discovery, we were unearthing more about ourselves, as well as others. We thought we were simply taking Latin and Greek, but, as it turned out, Latin and Greek were taking us—taking us to new places, insights, and perspectives.

Many times, when we step inside a new place, a new class, or a new book, we wind up learning something we never anticipated.

This is precisely the surprise that awaits us when we step inside the old place, the old book, that for many of us is nevertheless "new": the Scriptures of Israel. Like me and my classmates back in undergrad, we may think we're entering Genesis or Psalms or Isaiah to learn about God or history or poetry. And indeed, we do. But one of the surprises that comes along as we stroll with Adam through Eden, stand alongside Moses in the desert, and suffer with David in the Psalms, is that we begin to plumb the depths of *who we are*. New and beautiful vistas open up—as well as new, deep, dark, and frightening caverns. In a slow and steady journey through the Torah, Prophets, and writings of Israel, we often learn as much about ourselves as we do about God.

Jewish scholar Abraham Heschel was onto something when he wrote, "The Bible is not man's theology but God's anthropology."[1] The Bible is not our speculation about God but God's revelation of us and to us. He certainly tells us much about himself, including his identity, his wisdom, and his ways. But he also opens our eyes to see who we are as those crafted in his image.

The Bible is just as much (or more!) about humanity as it is divinity. Indeed, God's greatest revelation of who he is, is also in humanity—the humanity of Jesus. The divine image who made man is himself made man. Thus, an exploration of the Scriptures is also an exploration of the human heart, the human body, and human relationships. And among those relationships is friendship.

Privatized Humanity

To read the opening two chapters of Genesis is also to read the opening two insights into the nature of humanity. First, we are perfectly formed in the image of God—men and women. In him, we are complete. We are fearfully and wonderfully made. God created us as his children, the receptacles of his gifts. And those gifts he bestowed in spades. That is the first insight.

The second, unexpected insight into our nature is that, despite God's perfect formation of man, aloneness is un-good for man. In a narrative full of "goods" and "very goods," this is the first "not good" that we encounter (Gen. 2:18). It is not good for the man to be alone precisely because he is not created to live as an isolated, self-contained, self-sufficient, self-actuating, self-identifying individual. There are no islands in the stream of humanity. Even as there are three persons of the Trinity, distinguished in person, united in essence, so in the divine-image-bearing humanity there is a plurality of persons.

We are all inextricably united, not only by a shared nature but by shared parents. Every tiny, outwardly different twig on the vast tree of humanity—male or female, whatever race, whatever culture, whatever religion—is generated from one seed, one root. In that sense, when I, a white, male, American Christian, for instance, meet a black, female, African Muslim, I experience a two-person family reunion. I am face-to-face with my sister. The church rightly sings, "In Adam we have all been one, One huge rebellious man."[2] There is thus zero place in our oneness as a "one huge . . . man" for toes to feel uppity around elbows, or shoulders to gloat over buttocks. Racism, along with any–ism that denigrates, subjugates, or relegates a fellow human "below me," is a denial of, and slap in the face of, creation.

The same goes for individualism, which is the kissing cousin to racism. Both communicate the same error: I have zero intrinsic need of another. I am my own oasis in the desert of humanity. I may use you, but I don't need you. We are not on the same plane. I am my own self-contained person, complete in myself, content in myself, operating in my own privatized humanity. Within my skin, inside my head, operating within my heart and soul, are all the necessities requisite for a fulfilled life. Any contact with another person—be that coworker, spouse, or friend—is completely utilitarian, not constitutive of what makes me, me. The walls of my ego are not porous. They allow for no movement in or out. One hundred percent of me is found inside me. Such is the error of our thinking.

This false perspective, in a million nuanced forms, is the air we breathe. But it is polluted air. It is certainly not the fresh, biblical oxygen pumped out by the scriptures of Israel. There we are exposed to a revolutionary new way of understanding who we are. It seems revolutionary, but it is actually a re-presentation, a recapturing of who we were made to be. Far from individuals operating in individual ways independent of others, the Old Testament sinks us into the lives, hearts, and souls of others—not by option but by nature. This is not a lifestyle choice; it is simply the reality of being human. To be human is to be in relationship.

We are born into the world marked by our physical connectedness to others. Every baby has a mother and father. From conception onward we understand who we are not by looking inward but by looking outward, into the face of another. We "find ourselves" by looking at and into family, friends, and neighbors. Their face is the mirror of our identity, their bodies our origin.

The same goes for marriage. When Adam saw Eve, he exclaimed, "This is now bone of my bones, and flesh of my flesh" (2:23 KJV). He was saying, "I see myself in another, in her. Here, in one not me, I nevertheless see me. In seeing her, I not only see myself, but I see the good I lacked in myself."

We generally assume this intimate, body language is applicable only to the one-flesh union of husband and wife. But it's not. This language of "bone and flesh" is used outside of marriage as well. For instance, Laban said to Jacob, "Surely you are my bone and my flesh" (Gen. 29:14 NKJV). Abimelech told all the leaders of Shechem, "Remember that I am your own flesh and bone" (Judges 9:2 NKJV). Later, all the tribes said to David, "We are your bone and your flesh" (2 Sam. 5:1 NKJV). David himself said of the elders of Israel, "You are my brothers; you are my bone and my flesh" (19:12 ESV; cf. v. 13). Although the marriage bond is certainly far more intimate a bodily union than what exists between brothers or tribes, nevertheless the concrete, fleshly unity remains. We see our bone and our flesh in the bones and flesh of those around us.

To be human, therefore, is the exact opposite of navel-gazing. It is face-gazing. It is looking into the countenance of another and beholding a reflection of who we are. Humanity is therefore a corporate reality.

David and Jonathan

This understanding of what it means to be human informs what it means to be a friend and to need friends. As important as they are for mutual conversation, encouragement, and consolation, on a deeper level friends keep us rooted in a genuinely *human* life—that is, a life in which we live outside ourselves, gladly caught up in the web of a another's life, where we can love and serve them in moments of self-forgetfulness.

We see something like a parable of this in the friendship of David and Jonathan. Shortly after David slew Goliath, he was brought before King Saul. The youth and the king spoke about who David was and what he had done. After David had finished the conversation with Saul, the king's son, Jonathan became united to David in a deep and abiding friendship.

> The soul of Jonathan was knit to the soul of David, and Jonathan loved him as his own soul. And Saul took him that day and would not let him return to his father's house. Then Jonathan made a covenant with David, because he loved him as his own soul. And Jonathan stripped himself of the robe that was on him and gave it to David, and his armor, and even his sword and his bow and his belt. (1 Sam. 18:1–4 ESV)

Much later, after the death of Jonathan and his father on the battlefield, David sang a lament in which he said of his friend, "I am distressed for you, my brother Jonathan; very pleasant have you been to me; your love to me was extraordinary, surpassing the love of women" (2 Sam. 1:26 ESV).

The language used to describe the bond between David and Jonathan is indicative not only of the intensity of their friendship but the way in which their friendship rooted them deeply in a life of love—that is, a life of being truly human.

Jonathan's soul was "knit" (Hebrew: *qashar*) to the soul of David. The basic meaning of this verb is to bind, to tie together, as a scarlet thread was tied (*qashar*) to the hand of Zerah, or Rahab tied (*qashar*) a piece of scarlet to her window (Gen. 38:28; Josh. 2:18). The same verb is used to describe how God's words are to be

qashar to the foreheads and hands of Israel (Deut. 6:8). By exten-
sion, then, it is applied to the knot of love that ties people together.
Jacob's soul was *qashar* to the soul of his youngest son, Benjamin
(Gen. 44:30), just as Jonathan's was to David. That Jonathan "loved
him as his own soul" is expressive of what this soul-*qashar* meant.
He saw in David a reflection of who he himself was. This recognition
pulled him outside himself and bound him to another. It simultaneously emptied and filled him: emptied himself of a life all about
him and filled him with the life of another. We see this emptying
out illustrated in his stripping off of his robe and weapons and giving them to David. What was his—his inward soul and his outward
possessions—became another's. Jonathan's friendship benefited not
only David but himself as well. He discovered in this friend who he
was: a love-giver, a gift-giver, one who empties himself into the life
and soul of a friend. In short, Jonathan's actions are an epiphany of
what it means to be truly human.

David's words of lamentation echo and reinforce Jonathan's
actions; they also take them to a higher level. His friend had been
very "pleasant" (Hebrew: *na'em*) to David. The root and derivatives
of this word are used to describe beauty, goodness, and kindness.
They're applied also to the God of Israel. His divine name is *na'im*
(Ps. 135:3). The psalmist wants to behold the *no'am* of the Lord in his
temple (Ps. 27:4). David saw in Jonathan one whose kindness and
pleasantness mirrored that of God himself. Moreover, Jonathan's love
for him was "extraordinary" (from the Hebrew verb *pala*). This root
is commonly used to describe wondrous divine acts that are beyond
our ability to grasp or understand. This love, David says, was greater
than the love of women. The love of a woman for a man, or a man
for a woman, is an extraordinary gift. It is frequently held up as a mirror of the love between God and his people. In David and Jonathan's
case, however, the bond of love between them was even higher than
what exists between a man and woman. It was, like divine actions,
pala. Wonderful. Extraordinary. Surpassing all expectation. As such,
this love of friends mirrored even more closely the love of God for
his people. Indeed, it was a gift from God, designed to enable David
and Jonathan to experience in their friendship an earthly reflection of the celestial love of Yahweh for Israel. And at the same time,
it was a gift for them so they could grow into the love-givers and

love-receivers they were made to be as those crafted in the image of the loving God.

In the friendship of David and Jonathan, therefore, the Lord has given us an example of what this bond between friends enacts in the two people. They are tied together in such a way that one's soul mirrors the other's. This mirroring pulls us out of ourselves. It shows us who we truly are. And in the reception of the love of another, we see too the love of God—the extraordinary, pleasant favor of Yahweh toward us.

A Fleeting Glimpse

When Luther comments on the separation of Abraham from Lot, an uncle from his nephew, he asks, "Who would not consider this a heavy cross and a great evil?" Lot had been not only a nephew but a friend to Abraham. And "a faithful friend is a great boon and a precious treasure in any situation in life" because we cannot face our struggles alone. "It remains a great advantage to have a brother with whom one can converse about religion and from which one can hear words of comfort." Indeed, Luther says, "I for my part consider the loss of all my possessions less important than that of a faithful friend."[3]

Luther speaks here in the same spirit as did David upon the death of Jonathan. Indeed, he voices what many of us have experienced at the loss of faithful friends. It is a heavy cross to bear and a great evil to experience. Because in the death of that friend, we die, too. Our souls are bound to the friend, as Jonathan's was to David.

So while they live, while they remain pleasant (*naʾem*) and extraordinary (*pala*) to us, while we are able to give ourselves in love to them, and they to us, let us treasure these friendships for what they are: divine epiphanies of the love that the friend of sinners has for us. They are also, at the same time, divine epiphanies of who we are created to be. We are those who are most ourselves when we are outside ourselves. When our souls are not bound up inside us but bound to the soul of a friend. When we see in their faces a reflection of who we are. When we understand that we are not isolated humans, operating in a hermetically sealed cubicle of individuality, but members of one another. We are one body of humanity, even as the church is one body of Christ.

In being friends who love, and in receiving the love of friends, we catch a fleeting glimpse, through the darkness and fog of a fallen world, into the clear and bright air of the Eden that was and the Eden that will be at the consummation of the ages.

Friendship in the New Testament

Caleb E. Keith

I always get a little bit nervous when I see book or chapter titles like "Friendship in the New Testament." This is because the exploration of topics concerning human relationship—whether that be friendship, marriage, parenthood, or even politics—often turns into proof texting select or proverbial verses to create a checklist or method to living a better life. That is not to say that the New Testament does not speak about human relationships; it does both and directly and indirectly. However, when examining texts, it is absolutely necessary to ask what the author's stated purpose or goal is. While the New Testament is a collection of twenty-seven separate books written by eight separate authors, they all share a common stated goal: to describe, teach, and proclaim the Gospel of Jesus Christ. Everything contained within these books either affects that Gospel or is affected by it. So, if one looks at friendship in the New Testament, it is not enough to skim for examples of good friends or platitudes about friendship. Instead, it is necessary to explore the question: What purpose or place does friendship serve in light of the Gospel of Christ? My goal in this chapter is to explore the idea of friendship in the New Testament, dissecting it with the Gospel to better understand what it actually means to be a friend.

The word typically translated as friend in the New Testament is *philos*. It shares a linguistic root with the word *philia*, which is one of the ancient Greek words for love and is where we get the concept of "brotherly love." For the purposes of this chapter, it is important to note that *philos* and its various forms only occur a total of thirty-three times in the entire New Testament. Of those thirty-three, twenty-six are contained within the four Gospels, and twenty-three are spoken directly by Jesus, primarily in the parables. Outside of these explicit uses of the word *friend*, we also see examples of friendship among various New Testament figures such as Lazarus and Jesus, Paul and Barnabas, and Paul and Timothy. In this chapter, I will start by looking at two parables from Luke, the parable of the banquet and the parable of the prodigal son. Following this, I will examine the relationship between Paul and Timothy. The aim is to see the parables as a corrective lens or baseline to our way of thinking regarding sin, grace, and friendship, and additionally, to see an example of this mindset worked out between believers.

Jesus' use of the word *friend* is almost exclusively found as part of telling parables. These compact stories, which Jesus tells over the course of his entire ministry, share common themes and structures. Jesus used these parables to challenge cultural expectations. In them, he describes the kingdom and grace of God. Parables help realign what is a misguided view of the law, grace, and the hearer's status before God. When Jesus describes the kingdom of God, especially toward the end of his ministry, he talks about a party. Chapters 14 and 15 of the Gospel of Luke are a prime example of this. In 14, Jesus tells the story of the Great Banquet followed by the parable of the Prodigal Son in chapter 15. Along with a celebration, each of these stories includes friends or guests. While friendship is not the central topic, their inclusion presents a consistent typology. In particular, what stands out is that friends are in some fashion equals, called together for celebration. The question is, by what standard are friends considered equal?

When I think about an unexpected party, the first thing that comes to mind is a surprise birthday party. Friends and family organize and gather together unbeknownst to the lucky birthday boy or girl. As that person comes home, all the friends jump out and yell surprise! Then, the party commences. Yet this party really isn't all that unexpected; after all, there is an expected occasion to celebrate. What makes it unexpected is simply that one person was left in the dark. The parties that Jesus describes are just the opposite. They are unexpected by all except one person. There is no reason for these parties. In one, honored guests decline the invitation, so others are invited in their place; in the other, a reckless father kills his prized calf, celebrating the return of a son who wished him dead. In fact, as shown at the end of the prodigal son, these parties are so uncalled for and bizarre that they cause some people to become angry.

The story of the Great Banquet is prefaced by what at first seems like a proverbial statement from Jesus. He says, "When you give a dinner or a banquet, do not invite your friends or your brothers or your relatives or rich neighbors, lest they also invite you in return and you be repaid. But when you give a feast, invite the poor, the crippled, the lame, the blind, and you will be blessed, because they cannot repay you" (Luke 14:12–14 ESV). He then starts the parable by setting the scene. A party has been fully prepared, the guests have been invited, and soon the celebration will commence. There is just one problem. As the guests are called into the banquet, "they all alike began to make excuses. The first said to him, 'I have bought a field, and I must go out and see it. Please have me excused.' And another said, 'I have bought five yoke of oxen, and I go to examine them. Please have me excused.' And another said, 'I have married a wife, and therefore I cannot come'" (Luke 12:18–20 ESV). Every friend who was invited rejects his seat at the feast. One by one, they all have something better to do. So, the master of the banquet reaches out to those who have earned no place at the party. His servant goes out and gathers "the poor and crippled and blind and lame" (Luke 12:21 ESV). Unexpected guests are now the benefactors of a party that they have no business attending.

The mistake to be made here in analyzing this parable for the purpose of defining friendship is to consider ourselves the master of the party, the initial guests as friends who disappoint us, and the poor and the sick as those friends Jesus wants us to have. We have a much more meager role to play in this parable. God is always the one with the authority and the right to throw a party. He is also the only with the power to invite the poor, sick, and unworthy guests. That leaves us as either those who reject God's call or as sick, blind, and poor beggars. Neither option is flattering. What this parable forces us to recognize is that both the wealthy property owners and the poor beggars are equals. There is nothing either party does to earn their place at the table. It is simply the call of the master that makes one a guest. As Capon states, "The point is that none of the people who had a right to be at a proper party came, and that all the people who came had no right whatsoever

to be there. Which means therefore, that the one thing that has nothing to do with anything is rights. The parable says that we are going to
be dealt with in spite of our deserving, not according to them."[1]

The parable of the Prodigal Son goes even further by contrast-
ing the disobedient with the honorable rather than the rich and
the poor. The parable opens to a son who wants his father dead so
he can gain his inheritance and be free from the law of his father's
home. The father grants his son's wish and gives both his sons their
inheritance and lets the younger leave the household. The hate-filled
son goes on his way to a far-off land. However, his plan to live free
backfires. He squanders his money and loses his property. And after
he has spent everything, a severe famine arises. To survive, he hires
himself and soon finds himself feeding pigs. The famine and his pov-
erty are so severe that he wishes his circumstances were equal to at
least the pigs. In his despair, the son eventually travels home, hoping
to be reinstated to his father's house as a servant so at the very least
he might have something to eat.

What he finds at home is astonishing. His father welcomes him
home with arms wide open, treating him with the highest honor, and
throwing the biggest celebration the family has ever seen. The faithful older brother is enraged and chastises his father, saying, "Look,
these many years I have served you. I never disobeyed your command, yet you never gave me a young goat that I might celebrate
with my friends" (Luke 15:29 ESV). He and his friends, those people
who he has deemed equal to him, are the ones who deserve a party,
not a disobedient son who squandered half of everything the family owns. Here the older son demonstrates friendship rooted in an
equality of status like that described by Jesus as those who can repay
you. On the contrary, the father shows that the older son has more in
common with his brother than he wants to admit. Everything they
have is a gift of their father, and their place in the household is not
about what they have earned, but that they have both been called to
the table.

Neither of the two parables are explicitly about friendship.
However, they reveal who we are and who our friends will be. We
are weak, dying, and disobedient sinners. What we need is the word
of the Father calling us home despite our sin. Friends are equal to us
not because of earned status but because they too are poor, miserable

sinners in need of grace. Friends are also those explicitly equipped to call us inside. That is, they take up the role of the servant who is sent out to bring the word of the master to those outside the feast. So, friendship is in part made up by a recognition of sin, but even more it is defined by forgiveness of that sin, extending the call of the Father to come join the party. The word is always delivered on the lips of another, and as friends we are called to recognize our need to be brought inside and the need of those around us to whom we can deliver Good News.

Friends are people of mutual need. Both those rich cohorts who rejected the invitation to the party as well as the poor and miserable require something from outside themselves. They all need the grace of God delivered through his calling word. Apart from that grace, friends can only share in misery. They lack the comfort and rejoicing that comes with sharing in the Gospel. The Gospel changes friendship by empowering the forgotten and the lost to become servants of the master who are called to go out and bring more people into the party. We share a common nature as sinners. This means that we also share in the common need for the Gospel. It is the comfort of the Gospel that makes friendship truly powerful.

We see the especially through the example of Paul and Timothy. What we know about their relationship is given to us in two letters Paul wrote to encourage Timothy as he took up the role of leading a church. These epistles cover a broad range of topics; however, they are predominantly formed by consolation and encouragement. Throughout 1 and 2 Timothy, Paul continually warns Timothy of the various obstacles he will face when preaching the Gospel, including attacks for proclaiming the risen Christ. The vocation of friend helps sustain believers through these attacks and doubts. In 2 Timothy, Paul himself expresses great need for Timothy to minister back to him when he states:

Do your best to come to me soon. For Demas, in love with this present world, has deserted me and gone to Thessalonica. Crescens has gone to Galatia, Titus to Dalmatia. Luke alone is with me. Get Mark and bring him with you, for he is very useful to me for ministry. Tychicus I have sent to Ephesus. When you come, bring the cloak that I left with Carpus at Troas, also the books, and above all the parchments. Alexander the coppersmith did me great harm; the Lord will repay him according to his deeds. Beware of him yourself, for he strongly opposed our message. At my first defense no one came to stand by me, but all deserted me. May it not be charged against them! But the Lord stood by me and strengthened me, so that through me the message might be fully proclaimed, and all the Gentiles might hear it. So, I was rescued from the lion's mouth. The Lord will rescue me from every evil deed and bring me safely into his heavenly kingdom. To him be the glory forever and ever. Amen. (2 Tim. 4:9–18 ESV)

Paul could rely on Timothy to proclaim the Gospel to him in his greatest hour of need. While Timothy could not free him from prison or protect him from bodily suffering, he could preach back to him the word he first handed off to Timothy: "If we have died with him, we will also live with him; if we endure, we will also reign with him; if we deny him, he also will deny us; if we are faithless, he remains faithful—for he cannot deny himself" (2 Timothy 2:11–13).

A friend is not just someone we like talking to and playing golf with on the weekend. The New Testament shows us that our best friends are those who recognize our sin and brokenness because they know their own, and seeing such sin, they extend the call of the Father out to us so that we to can take part in the great celebration. This is not to say one cannot or should not have non-Christian friends. In fact, the opposite is true. It is our calling as servants in Christ to bring the Gospel to those waiting outside, even if they, like the wealthy invitees or the angry son, refuse to come in. New Testament friendship is about equality, yet not an earned equality of status or likability but rather an equality of need. We are the poor, the sick, and the lame who cannot come to the kingdom of God by our own accord. We need to be continually called to it. And at the same time, as believers who in Christ belong to the kingdom of God, we are sent out to comfort and call those closest to us so they too might rejoice in the comfort that is the Gospel.

The Invisible Bond of Friendship from Gilgamesh to Augustine

Daniel van Voorhis, PhD

Friendship is a station in life—and one of some consequence—but it is without rites or ceremonies. This causes it to be underrepresented in histories, underappreciated as a relationship, and generally understudied for its own sake. Despite being hard to define and the lack of official formalities, friendship has offered much inspiration for ancient storytellers. Must not "a history of friendship" exist then? In 2003, Allan Bray published *The Friend*, a historical account of friendship that began with the author investigating the practice of monks being buried together. It was named the 2004 book of the year by *History Today*. Although narrow in scope, the book opened the practice and concept to further historical study. Unfortunately, Bray's book was published posthumously as he died while it was in its final editing stages. When he was finishing the book, he too lamented the lack of good historical research on friendship.

Perhaps a primary reason why there are no authoritative books on the history of friendship is that friendships are rarely the only bond that ties people together. Even something like denominational affiliation can mark out a relationship on more certain terms than a nebulous friendship based on "mere" affection.

I have made the choice to only look at male friendship in the premodern Western world to limit the field of inquiry and thereby making a study of this type manageable for a collection of essays. By trade I am a modern historian, and thus I put myself at a disadvantage when looking at the premodern world. It is not my normal stomping grounds. Nonetheless, I believe the benefits of focusing on antiquity outweigh the drawbacks. By sticking to the premodern world, we greatly reduce the number of possible texts and sources. A smaller sample size is helpful, but so too is a more concentrated audience.

Imagine trying to tell the story of American primetime television viewing patterns in 2018. Streaming? Tivo'ed? How many of the channels on how many platforms would you have to chase down? Twenty shows might get a million viewers each, and there is no clear majority. Now imagine telling the same story, but about American television watching habits in the 1980s when any hit show could regularly reach 20 million viewers on any given night. With only three major channels, we can take the temperature of the viewing audience by observing, say, themes in *MASH*, *Cheers*, and *Dynasty*. While we might not be able to reach the level of analysis we could with numerous outlets, we are nevertheless observing a very similar people group funneled into fewer groups. So, by looking at a few stories from the ancient and medieval world, we can see the ancient and medieval world that they both interpreted and reflected to some extent. This will allow us to look at the broad Western canon for stories we can assume were meaningful or at least read/heard by a majority of the people.

Any origins question like, "Where did _____ come from?" sends us back to our ancient texts. Different texts carry different levels of authority, and they can clash with each other at times. That is to say, we don't need to be biased against or toward old texts. The idea isn't that these texts are better because they are ancient but rather they are worth what they might bring in terms of actual etiologies (stories about how things started), or they explore themes that have proven to pass the test of time. The most widely read ancient texts are, of course, the Jewish and Christian Scriptures. But another ancient text, that of *The Epic of Gilgamesh*, says something in particular to the ancient world and the idea of friendships.

The story of Gilgamesh comes from a Mesopotamian poem dating to about 2000 BC. Gilgamesh, a being part divine and part human, was the mightiest king with the greatest city filled with the tallest buildings. He was also a successful king but not a very good one. As Gilgamesh grew in stature, he began taking virgin brides on their wedding night to his own bed first. This caused the people to cry out to the gods and ask for relief. So the gods created another divine/human being who, while fully uncivilized, would come to rescue the people. This being, Enkidu, lived among the beasts until he slept with a prostitute and was thus awakened to his humanity. As he transitioned from beastly to civilized life, the texts says, "becoming aware of himself, he sought a friend."

Once he found himself in a state of civilization, he knew he needed companionship, and friendship was likely the most expedient way to achieve that. But first, Enkidu confronted Gilgamesh over the taking of the brides, and they clashed in an epic battle through the streets of Uruk. Through their combat, however, Gilgamesh became the friend Enkidu sought. They joined forces and soon began felling trees from sacred forests and defying the gods. For this, Enkidu had to die, and the remainder of the story is about Gilgamesh trying to find the key to everlasting life to raise his friend from the dead. Ultimately, after meeting with a Noah-esque character, Gilgamesh descends into a lake to retrieve a life-giving flower. He retrieves the flower, but the story ends with it being stolen by a crafty snake, and thus the friendship was not able to be rekindled.

The bond between these two heroes, their physicality and masculinity, is on display throughout the epic. Amid their friendship, they learn more about each other while learning about life, the gods, and mortality. For an ancient text, with a very different context to ours, one can still hear the agony in the mourning words of Gilgamesh:

> I am going to die!—am I not like Enkidu?!
> Deep sadness penetrates my core,
> I fear death, and now roam the wilderness
> I will set out to the region of Utanapishtim, son of Ubartutu, and will
>   go with utmost dispatch!
> Six days and seven nights I mourned over him
> and would not allow him to be buried
> until a maggot fell out of his nose.
> I was terrified *by his appearance*,
> I began to fear death, and so roam the wilderness.[1]

The ancient Near Eastern world, in both biblical and extra-biblical material, showed a keen eye toward this kind of suffering, and would often use funerals as the only appropriate time for the relationship to be memorialized in speech. As an example, Homer's *Iliad* features the friendship between Patroclus and Achilles as one of its primary themes. While other relationships are portrayed, the relationship between these two men is used to enunciate the virtue of loyalty and pain of grief while also illustrating metaphysic of friendship in the afterworld. While it is Achilles's rage that propels the story from the beginning, his mourning at the death of Patroclus humanizes him. Upon the death of Patroclus, who fought in Achilles's stead and was slain by Hector, Achilles bereaves in a manner reminiscent of Gilgamesh.

> My dear comrade's dead—Patroclus—the man I loved beyond all other comrades, loved as my own life—I've lost him. . . . My spirit rebels—I've lost the will to live, to take my stand in the world of men—unless, before all else, Hector's battered down by my spear and gasps away his life, the blood-price for Patroclus.[2]

But the bereavement, while a central part of the story, is only half the story. Homer includes a curious bit after his death, when Patroclus is in the afterlife, mourning his relationship with the living.

> Sleeping, Achilles? You've forgotten me, my friend. You never neglected me in life, only now in death. Bury me, quickly—let me pass the Gates of Hades. They hold me off at a distance, all the souls, the shades of the burnt-out, breathless dead, never to let me cross the river, mingle with them . . . Oh give me your hand—I beg you with my tears![3]

This is not so odd when you consider the classical Greek metaphysics of friendship. There is something semidivine, heroic, and noble but also deeply spiritual to it.

A similar sentiment is found in Plato's *Symposium*.

> And when one of [the friends] meets with his other half, the actual half of himself, whether he be a lover of youth or a lover of another

sort, the pair are lost in an amazement of love and friendship and intimacy, and one will not be out of the other's sight, as I may say, even for a moment: these are the people who pass their whole lives together; yet they could not explain what they desire of one another. For the intense yearning which each of them has toward the other does not appear to be the desire of lover's intercourse, but of something else which the soul of either evidently desires and cannot tell, and of which she has only a dark and doubtful presentiment.[4]

The significance of friendship in all of these forms carried this theme through the classical world and into the Roman world, but its dearth was also picked up by no less than Cicero.

Both in our public and private lives he and I have shared all the same interests. We lived in the same home; we soldiered together in the field. Our tastes and aims and views were identical—and that is where the essence of a friendship must always lie. Then he alludes directly to the history of Greek male friendships, especially as manifest in such doubles as Achilles and Patroclus: The hope which I cherish all the more keenly because, throughout the whole course of history, the pairs of friends who have been lastingly remembered only amount to barely three or four at the very most.[5]

Thus, friendship from the earliest days of recorded thought through the age of the late Roman Republic understood friendship as a profoundly spiritual yet elusive bond. The concept is still elusive to us today in our inability to properly categorize, memorialize, or otherwise commemorate it. While many rabbis rightly point to the story of Jonathan and David from the book of 1 Samuel as the centerpiece for Hebraic tradition, Jesus famously eschewed family (let the dead bury themselves!) in favor of likeminded friends and called for a group of disciples to be devoted to the cause. While the religious initiation practices helped to cement the relationships between the individuals and the church, it is good to remember that these formal relationships grew out of the informal relationship of friendship. This friendship based on service and sacrifice was encapsulated by Jesus, who proclaimed: "greater love has no one than this, to lay down his life for his friends" (John 15:13). The community born out of Christ's death as a sacrifice for his friends (the whole world) after this event would not only call each other "brother" and "sister" but also "friend" as a term of revolutionary equality.

It is no surprise, then, that the Christian church would be on the vanguard of defining and defending friendship. The great theologian Augustine of Hippo cemented the place of this mystical and spiritual relationship of friendship when he wrote upon the death of a friend:

> to talk and laugh and do kindnesses to each other; to read pleasant books together; to make jokes together and then talk seriously together. . . . These and other similar expressions of feeling, which proceed from the hearts of those who love and are loved in return, and are revealed in the face, the voice, the eyes, and in a thousand charming ways, were like kindling fire to melt our souls together and out of many to make us one. It is this which we love in our friends.[6]

As the man who was perhaps most responsible for introducing a blend of Christian and platonic thought, it is of no surprise that Augustine went on to write, "I felt that my soul and my friend's had been one soul in two bodies," recalls *The Symposium*.[7]

A true friendship seems to be rooted in experience and existential awareness. That is, other relationships seem to grow up and around friendship based on who we are, where we live, and what we believe. But undoing the threads to see which relationship corresponds to what particular action or feeling might be impossible. As the Middle Ages dawned, friendship would be revered even if less than understood and was carried forth by Christians, mostly male and mostly monks. The very topic of these intense relationships became the subject of Bray's aforementioned award-winning book. The Christian notion of friendship, taking on metaphysical components alluded to in other great works, would come to be a well-trod and understood trope across the generations. Huck Finn and Tom Sawyer and, later, Ross and Rachel, embody this deep relationship sometimes based on nothing but a shared belief in the invisible world, but the significance of friends is undeniable.

Friendship is an under-noticed force in the flow of human history, and while we have recognized its power since ancient times, without a ceremony or rite, it is underappreciated. We see death as a strange component to so many of these friendships, and funeral orations of various sorts make up the majority of our sources. What is it about a death that causes reflection on this particular relationship? Other kinds of relationships do not suffer from lack of notice at funerals, but it is the one ceremony at which proclamations of friendship are found more than anywhere else. Perhaps it is the inviolability and uncertainness of death that causes a deep reflection on the nature of all our human relationships with their power and frailty. A broader historical approach or personal reflection would likely reproduce these findings from antiquity. An appraisal of our friendships, before the grave, and a desire to have others as beneficial relations is positive and should be reinforced through the stories we tell, our theologies, and the recognition we give it in our day-to-day lives.

The Philosophy of Friendship

Daniel Deen, PhD

Plato famously declared in the *Republic* that the most important question of philosophy is "how we ought to live." At the center of his philosophical program was a commitment to the examined life, a life spent in pursuit of truth, goodness, and beauty. Plato's most faithful student, friend, and critic, Aristotle, followed in Plato's footsteps regarding the ultimate aim of living life well. His treaties on virtue and excellent living included two chapters on the nature of friendship. He saw in friendship, as did Plato, something essential to living life well. This sentiment runs throughout the entire philosophical tradition. None other than C.S. Lewis in the twentieth century, responding to contemporary concerns concerning the Darwinian machine, footnoted Plato and Aristotle when he wrote, "Friendship is unnecessary, like philosophy, like art . . . It has no survival value; rather it is one of those things that gives value to survival."[1]

While this volume investigates Lewis's comments on friendship in several places, this chapter examines the general philosophical view of friendship expressed in Plato and his pupil Aristotle. The task is to set before us an image of what friendship is and its relationship to the good life. Then I will juxtapose the philosophical image of friendship with the thought of Martin Luther and his placement of Christian friendship, what he calls the "mutual consolation of the brethren," within the office of the keys.

My basic goal in this chapter is twofold. First, I will illustrate that the classical conception of friendship shares certain common themes that are easily recognized in the sorts of friendships we desire to maintain today. Second, I will argue that Luther's placement of friendship within the office of the keys reminds us of the complete reversal of wisdom that is the Christian message. The secular philosophers have much to say about friendship and testify to the greatness of friendship, but they all fall short of grounding friendship in anything surviving the temporal.

Plato and Aristotle: Methods and Aims

A good place to begin an investigation into the style and thought of Plato and Aristotle is sixteenth-century Italy. Around 1511, the Apostolic Palace in the Vatican received its second commissioned painting by Rafael, *The School of Athens*. This fresco places two figures at the center. Both are locked in argument, with one pointing into the heavens and the other pointing toward the earth. The man surveying the celestial is Plato, while the man examining the terrestrial is Aristotle. A teacher and his pupil both agreed as to the value of philosophy but disagreed as to the nature and practice of it. Both started competing schools exposing the differences between their thought. Rafael represents the influence of their thought through the figures to the right of Plato and left of Aristotle. These figures, like soldiers in a company, flank their champion and represent the various philosophers operating within the tradition of their fearless leader.

It is safe to say that both Plato and Aristotle agreed the aim of philosophy was to garner wisdom. Wisdom entailed living the virtuous life and ultimately a life of happiness, happiness being the loose translation of a thick concept captured by the Greek word *eudaemonia*. I'll return to this concept in my discussion of Aristotle. For now, *eudaemonia* may be captured in the dying words of twentieth-century philosopher Ludwig Wittgenstein. While breathing his last breaths in a cancer-ridden body, it is reported that he told his friend, the philosopher Norman Malcolm, that he "had a wonderful life."[2] This notion of a "wonderful life" or a life well-lived is the essence of what it means to live a life of *eudaemonia*.

Platonic and Aristotelian philosophies both aimed at a life of *eudaemonia*, but their methods of attaining it differed. The differences are directly linked to the celestial or terrestrial orientation captured in Rafael's painting. Plato's heavenly gaze is associated with a more rationalist school of thought. This rationalism held that minds could transcend the physical world in search of eternal truths that define the very physical objects stubbing our toes on earth. Meanwhile, Aristotle's terrestrial stance is given over to a more empirical approach to philosophy. In contradistinction from Plato, Aristotle thought that all knowing, understanding, and wisdom begin in sense-experience. The mind cannot fathom that which it cannot touch, taste, smell, hear, or see. As we shall see in the next two sections, these methodological differences deeply influence the way that both Plato and Aristotle analyze the concept of friendship.

Plato on Friendship

The first complete philosophical work devoted to friendship in the Western philosophical tradition is Plato's *Lysis*. Do not let the term *complete* lead you astray. There is nothing complete about this dialogue in relation to the concept of friendship. In fact, no answer is given as to the nature of friendship. In typical Platonic fashion, the dialogue abruptly ends after raising a handful of potential definitions and showing various ways in which the given definitions are problematic. A further oddity about the dialogue is its setting. The entire conversation takes place under the pretense that Socrates is illustrating for a fellow young man how to get little boys at the gym to love him. These two points, as disconnected as they first may appear, provide the background to much, if not all, philosophical rumination on friendship to follow, even unto the twenty-first century.

I'll begin by discussing the more awkward of my two points, which is the pederast undertones of the dialogue. Socrates often makes offhand comments about the beauty of his interlocutors and younger boys in general. The offhandedness is disregarded and directly analyzed in three specific dialogues concerning the nature of love—*Lysis*, *Symposium*, and the *Phaedrus*. The *Symposium* and *Phaedrus* are given over to conversations regarding *eros* (sexual love), while the *Lysis* concerns itself with *philo* (brotherly love).

Socrates himself devotes a significant portion of the *Symposium* to justifying his decision not to engage in physical relations with a particularly handsome adolescent named Alcibiades. For Socrates, physical love was but a shadow or representation of a more divine love. In fact, the physical often hindered the mind's ascent to the heavenly realm of goodness, truth, and beauty. Thus, in the *Lysis*, the whole conversation shaped around how to properly talk and make little boys love you was in direct opposition to the more sexual connotations often associated with pederasty. Hippothales, the character who desires the love of Lysis, fails because he does not engage the mind of Lysis. Socrates scolds Hippothales for swelling the boy's emotions, a decidedly physical component of humanity, with love songs and poems. True friendship, according to Plato, is one that takes place through engaging the mind, not the body.

While the dialogue is a revolt against the more appalling characteristics of pederasty, the central theme is to define the nature of friendship. In fact, it is an illustration of good friendship. The central problem of the dialogue is how to understand the love that is involved between friends. Over and over again questions are raised as to the directionality of love between friends. Must true friends love reciprocally? Can one be a friend if the love is not returned? What about the likeness of individuals? If two people share in characteristics or attributes, can they really love one another, as they will not have anything to offer to the other? Is utility a defining characteristic of friendship? These questions drive the platonic dialogue, serving to illustrate how difficult it is to provide a definition of friendship. The difficulty is due to the fact that Plato requires a very demanding sort of definition. Let us call the sort of definition that Plato demands a Platonic Definition.

A Platonic Definition is a set of jointly sufficient and necessary conditions that capture all actual instances of friendship. It is in the search for definition that Plato tips his hand toward rationalism. His desired definition is a formal definition that ought to categorize the essential form of a concept such as friendship. This form then provides the rule by which we can measure the physical manifestations of friendship we experience. It is the standard by which we take our friendships, hold them to the form in Plato's heaven, and make a judgment as to the truth or falsity of our actual friendships. In his own words, "When we talk about all the things that are our friends . . . it is clear that we are merely using the word 'friend'. The real friend is surely that in which all these so-called friendships terminate."[3]

The problem is that these definitions remained elusive to Plato. The closest examples that Plato gives of a perfect definition are mathematical in nature (e.g., triangle = three-sided figure, the sum of the interior angles equaling 180 degrees). Notice how the definition does not point to any one triangle but to all possible triangles. This is because the perfect triangle denoted by the definition resides in the nonphysical realm of the forms, only understandable through the mind. Mathematics became the default example of the sort of definition Plato was searching for when he analyzed a concept. If you think back to geometrical proofs in high school, you'll get a sense of how Plato operated. Given certain formal or axiomatic definitions, you could deduce further truths that necessarily followed from the given definitions. Plato was after those given definitions, the forms that all reality, including social reality, were deduced from. The problem, however, is that mathematical precision with concepts such as friendship seems problematic. Plato meandered through countless dialogues attempting to define concepts mathematically, resulting in much frustration when the definitions were not forthcoming. This is why many dialogues such as the *Lysis* end flat. Every axiomatic definition provided for friendship ends with potential counterexamples and contradictions.

The philosophical import of this dialogue is not, however, found in its uprooting traditional Greek norms of pedophilia, nor its inability to define friendship. The dialogue itself is an illustration of friendship and the potential friendship has for Plato's view of the good life. I've already mentioned that Plato valued the mind more than the body. Friendship is about love of the mind, not the physical. Friends, for Plato, therefore, are much more means to a further end of contemplating the forms than simple fishing or knitting companions. A good friend will be able to open the heavens to you, and as is discussed in Plato's other dialogue about erotic love, the *Symposium*, a friend will help birth philosophical ideals that are closer to true reality than anything this side of heaven. Friendship is necessary to the good life only in so far as it stretches your mind, providing a glimpse of truth, goodness, and beauty.

Aristotle on Friendship

Plato's concern with friendship was always with necessary and sufficient conditions and how conversation regarding those conditions lifted us from the mundane to the celestial. Aristotle, our empiricist, brought friendship back to earth. Aristotle noticed that Plato's view was a bit too formal and utilitarian to adequately capture the nature of friendship. Aristotle recognized that friends do make us better people, but he interpreted Plato to be arguing that true friends are only those who can elevate our minds to the realm of heavenly forms. Aristotle recognized that the simple pleasures of companionship, the physical enjoyment of being surrounded by, in conversation with, and working together with likeminded people, is also a good. Aristotle broke with Plato's attempt to perfectly define friendship, opting instead to describe friendship. His major discussion of friendship occupies two chapters of his book on practical philosophy called the *Nicomachean Ethics*. He offers a descriptive picture of friendship as it was actually found in the city-states of ancient Greece. In short, he asserts that humankind is social, binding together into communities, in hopes of securing a life of happiness.

Happiness is an important aspect of Aristotelian ethical and political thought. Happiness is the English translation of the Greek word *eudaemonia*. Happiness, however, is a misleading translation as the contemporary ear often associates happiness with the subjective feeling of happiness. Aristotle, in concert with Plato, viewed happiness as the state of living life well. A more accurate translation is something akin to well-being. *Eudaemonia*, then, is that state of living life well or human flourishing. In this sense, to be human is to strive to live the most excellent life possible—that is, according to Aristotle, a life of rationality in accord with virtue.

The aim of life is to attain Aristotelian happiness, and the ultimate end of every human action is in service to attaining happiness. Friendship is a part of this picture as we voluntarily enter into relationships with others.

So, what is a friend according to Aristotle? How does friendship fit into the Aristotelian picture of the happy life? As mentioned earlier, Aristotle does not opt for platonic definitions. Rather, he attempts to synthesize actual observations of friendships in the world. These Aristotelian definitions are more similar to what social scientists call operational definitions. The definitions do not promise necessary and sufficient conditions but functionally descriptive definitions. Thus, as Aristotle looked at the various ways we love those we describe as friends he notes, "Now these reasons differ from each other in kind; so, therefore do the corresponding forms of love and friendship. There are therefore three kinds of friendship, equal in number to the things that are lovable; for with respect to each there is a mutual and recognized love, and those who love each other wish well to each other in that respect in which they love one another."[4] Aristotle recognized three different uses of the term love involved in friendship. These are loves and consequently friendships of utility, pleasure, and character.

Friendships of utility are based upon an expected return on investment. These are the basis of good business relationships. In our digital age, most of our economic exchanges are done with little to no time spent talking with the people we make transactions with. But the idea behind a friendship of utility is that your local baker, butcher, or candlestick maker must be friendly if you are to transact business with him or her. The friendships, however, are predicated upon the basis of need. You and I will be friends as long as we sustain each other's needs—in other words, so long as we maintain a simple utility to each other. This is the most basic form of friendship for Aristotle and, in some sense, is the basic civic friendship that makes civil society possible.

Friendships of pleasure are those that are purely engaged on the basis of emotions of happiness. These friendships are expressed in social settings where we genuinely enjoy the company of others, but only in so far as we feel pleasure. These are related to the friendships of utility in which we receive a genuine good in return from being friendly with these people, but the good received is the subjective sense of happiness. We enjoy the quick wit of Johnny or the fantastic stories that Susan tells. Enduring friendships may develop, but the main motivation for these relationships is to simply enjoy each other's company. Due to the emotional nature of these friendships, they are as fickle as the friendships of utility. Aristotle sees friendships of pleasure as the most common sort of friendship, but it is the most brutish sort of friendship, appealing not to our rational human nature but our animal nature.

Friendships of character represent Aristotle's ideal of friendship. This is the virtuous friendship, where the friendship is based upon Aristotelian ethical principles of virtue. You love your friend simply for the person he or she is. There is no expectation of return on investment. There is not even an expectation of emotional happiness. Your love and beneficence are directed at the other simply because that person is the kind of person worth loving. It is not that utility and pleasure do not find their way into our more enduring character friendships; it is that they do not define them. Friendships of character are the most enduring and rare of friendships as there simply are not many people in the world, let alone people we actually come into contact with, who uphold the exacting Aristotelian standards of virtue. Nevertheless, there is something to Aristotle's notion of simply loving a friend for who he or she is, being attracted to his or her character apart from the utility or pleasure that person bring to our lives.

Plato and Aristotle: Lessons

What can be learned from these brief explorations of Plato and Aristotle on the nature of friendship? Focusing on the fundamental differences between the philosophers' thought on friendship masks important similarities. The first point of similarity is the insistence that good friends ought to make us better people. Plato thought that proper friends could elevate our minds to higher planes of existence, while Aristotle believed that friends provided the backdrop to measuring your own character. Regardless of the different ways they interpreted the aim of friendship, they agreed that friends are an essential component to the good life. Without friends, Platonic conversation and the development of virtue en route to the life of *eudaemonia* becomes close to impossible.

The second point of similarity is how difficult it is to find and maintain good friendships. Plato never truly came across another person capable of maintaining his intellectual fervor, and Aristotle's rigorous conception of virtue made good men few and far between. This is a problem that is prominent in future philosophical discourse on the nature of friendship from Cicero to Kant and beyond. The maintaining of appropriate sorts of friendships, and our human proclivity to weakness and vice, is always an empirical marker speaking against the conceivability of both Platonic and Aristotelian friendships. Anybody who has suffered at the hands of a supposed friend or has fallen in with the wrong sorts of friends understands how damaging friendship may be.

Third, both Plato and Aristotle suggest that friendship makes life worth living by giving us glimpses of what life could be. Every friendship comes with the hope that my life is better with this person in it. The friends we surround ourselves with, ignoring the second point of similarity above, help us to see a reality that is more true, good, and beautiful. Whether it is platonic glimpses of the ethereal or the Aristotelian grit of living excellently within the confines of society, both agree that friends help us see what is possible.

It is my contention that these underlying similarities in Plato and Aristotle ought to resonate with our own thinking about friendship. If we reflect on the friendships manifest in our lives, it is true that I have become a better person due to friends. Part of this becoming a better person is due to the eudaemonic glimpses of what life could be like when I am with friends. The world slows down, and life is simply better. Whether the time spent with friends leads to ethereal conversations of the way the world ought to be or the simple joking and lighthearted conversation that takes place within the terrestrial task of helping a friend paint a room, life together makes life worth living. Moreover, as any parent with children entering middle school and high school understands, the caveat of the dangers of friendship is very real. Good friends are hard to come by, and the maintaining of those relationships is nothing short of a miracle.

Christian Friendship

St. Augustine adroitly noted that his training in Greek thought, particularly through the lens of Neo-Platonism, provided a picture of the good life. But it lacked any discussion of grace and a life marked by repentance. He states, "So I began to read, and discovered that every truth I had read in those other books [philosophy] was taught here [St. Paul] also, but now inseparably from your gift of grace."[5] Augustine was discovering the biblical truth stated in texts such as 1 Corinthians 1:18, "For the message of the cross is foolishness to those who are perishing, but to us being saved it is the power of God." Augustine's conversion to Christianity marked a re-centering of the Christian life as one founded on Christ and his forgiveness. An Augustinian monk by the name of Martin Luther emphasized the same insight in the sixteenth century. Augustine was by all rights a professional rhetorician and philosopher as well as a theologian. Martin Luther claimed only that of theologian. However, that doesn't mean that the writings of Luther are not of philosophical import. In fact, I would argue that Luther has much to say to the philosophical enterprise. This closing section will briefly elucidate how Augustine's insight and Luther's placement of "the mutual consolation of the brethren" within the office of the keys reorients the ancient conception of friendship in such a way as to ground friendship in something more eternal than Plato could ever conceive and more corporeal than Aristotle ever thought possible.

Assuming that Luther's statement concerning the brethren is an expression of friendship, what follows from its location in the Smalcald Articles? The comment is found in a section of the Articles where Luther is explaining the power of the Gospel to forgive sinners. He equates the "mutual conversation and consolation" with the office of the keys. The office of the keys is the authority that the church in its official capacity has to bind and loose sins. It is the power that scripture grants to corporate confession and absolution to actually do what our confession and absolution says it does—forgive sins. Why would Luther then locate the "mutual conversation and consolation" within the office of the keys? Robert Kolb suggests that Luther was intentional about not separating the power of the keys from the priesthood of all believers.[6] The idea is that while a priestly hierarchy is important to the functioning of a church, they hold no special powers over the laity. When the pastor forgives my sins corporately at worship, the same effect is granted when my friend forgives me for my transgressions. This is all related to the Word of God working salvation and not anything I may bring to the table, but it is also a powerful recasting of the nature of the role of priests and common folk. Moreover, it has interesting implications for the philosophical nature of friendship.

Luther's insight is to turn the classical philosophical notion of what makes a friend on its head. Recall that both Plato and Aristotle believed that friendship was a necessary component to the good life, that friendships provided glimpses of an alternative reality, whether celestial or terrestrial. The movement, so to speak, was always upward, toward a better life. It also meant that true friendship was difficult to come by and maintain as virtuous agents are few and far between. Luther would agree that friends provide glimpses into the good life. However, the good life that Luther rediscovered in the Reformation was one grounded in the forgiveness of Christ. It was one that begins with the fear of the Lord and a righteous death and resurrection turning fear to joy. Therefore, the conception of friendship that arises in Luther's Smalcald comment is one that is not grounded in humans working toward the good life, but the good life handed to us from the cross. It is true that together with friends we catch glimpses of what life could be like, but our glimpses are not fickle hopes often left wanting like the end of Platonic dialogues. No, we rest assured in the mutual conversation and consolation of the brethren that our glimpses of what life could be like are rooted in the historical love that God pours out to us from the cross.

It is in this grounding of all existence in the forgiveness of Christ that all worldly philosophy stumbles. It is where the idolatry of our minds splinter at the cross of Christ, and it is where one finds true friends who share in an identity that transcends their individuality, uniting communities together through the blood of the Lamb. This is not to say that all are then friends or that our glimpses of what life on earth could be like are qualitatively better than the ancient philosophers conceived. We share in the joys and difficulties of friendship that Plato and Aristotle discussed. However, a qualitative difference arises in that the shadow of the cross is where friends finally land, not ethereal Platonic Definitions or terrestrial Aristotelian perfections. In Christ the heavens and the earth combine in the ultimate expression of human frailty: death. And with three simple words, "It is finished," the grandeur of the heavens exploded beyond anything Plato thought conceivable, and the physical world became more significant than Aristotle could ever have dreamed. Luther's insight was to locate friendship within this matrix of forgiveness, providing a foundation to friendship that will outlast any wisdom of the ancients.

The Ethics of Friendship

Jeffrey C. Mallinson, DPhil

The call of Jesus is a call to love everyone. Absolutely everyone. Christians, as ones invited to a new sort of life through unmerited grace, become the embodiment of Christ's nontransactional, self-giving presence in a world that is accustomed to pain, relational bean counting, and betrayal. Accordingly, in light of Jesus' call to love even one's enemies (Luke 6:27–36), the only substantial difference between an enemy and a friend is that an enemy is someone a Christian loves despite the pain caused by that relationship,[1] whereas a friend is someone a Christian loves *and also* evokes the joys of affection and camaraderie.

Granted, this way of speaking can be confusing in our cultural situation, since we tend to think of love as an intensification of friendship. For instance, we sometimes hear people say something like, "We're just friends" as a way to explain, "We aren't in love." Christians may still speak this way colloquially, of course, to avoid confusion.[2] Technically, however, Christians might rightly assume that to "like" someone or consider them a friend is to enjoy a more intimate and special relationship than the love we are called to have for all our neighbors. A Christian might love his or her spouse but not experience (at least for a time) a feeling of friendship. A joyous gift of Christian liberty, found only in the Gospel, is that we are free to be selective with respect to friendship. Just as we are free to pursue this or that way of serving our neighbor, we are likewise free to develop closer bonds with this or that particular neighbor.

In other words, Christian love is indiscriminate and universal (albeit difficult to embody), whereas Christian friendship is preferential and unevenly extended. Simply surrounding oneself with acquaintances is not the point of real friendship. As Proverbs 18:24 warns, "A man of many companions may come to ruin, but there is a friend who sticks closer than a brother."[3] This freedom to practice selectivity in friendship resonates with Luther's paradox, in his treatise *On the Freedom of the Christian*, wherein he states that a Christian is simultaneously a master and servant of all. As servants of all, we freely extend genuine and unconditional love to each person we encounter. As masters of all, we are free to maintain our personal boundaries, choose our confidants carefully, and decide how and when we spend time with our neighbors and colleagues. Indeed, the voluntary nature of friendship is precisely what makes it such a delightful gift. It exists through the power of mutual affection and values, rather than depending on a formal vow, a law, or even a divine injunction.

This chapter will explore the ethics of friendship, highlight ways in which virtue helps us choose the right friends, and consider ways in which friends are able to help each other reinforce Christian virtue. I will argue that, while friendship is not required of us in a particular case, it should remain nontransactional. That is, one ought not choose a friend solely on the basis of what that person might provide in terms of material or emotional benefits. Rather, when two individuals share a commitment to key virtues, they become close companions on a common path, in a shared mission, and with shared allegiances. As Augustine said:

> [T]he love involved in friendship ought to be gratuitous. I mean, the reason you have a friend, or love one, ought not to be so that he can do something for you; if that's why you love him, so that he can get you some money, or some temporal advantage, then you aren't really loving him, but the thing he gets for you. A friend is to be loved freely, for his own sake, not for the sake of something else.[4]

Ideally, friends share a common commitment to the Christian virtues of faith, hope, and love (1 Cor. 13:13). Friends work together to foster an ethos that encourages the pursuit of the three classic, transcendental values: goodness, truth, and beauty.

Virtue Ethics as the Ideal Normative Ethic in the Context of Friendship

Virtue is the only ethical theory that makes sense of genuine friendship. Philosophers call the exploration of the nature of good itself *meta-ethics*. That isn't our focus here. In the context of friendship, we are more interested in ethical theories related to making moral choices. This is called *normative* ethics. There are three basic approaches to normative ethics: (1) *deontology*, or duty-based ethics, which examines the nature of an act, (2) *consequentialism*, which considers the results of an action, and (3) *virtue theory* (also called personalism), which is concerned with the character of the person performing an act. I believe that a virtue-based ethic is the best way to approach normative ethics within the context of friendship.[5]

Deontology urges unequivocal allegiance to moral duties (e.g., the duty to never lie). Thus, if I should never lie, it hardly matters whether I'm speaking with a friend or an enemy. Deontology might prompt me to be a moral person toward a friend, but not *because* he or she is a friend. Likewise, consequentialism might offer a way of considering how my actions might positively or negatively affect the happiness of a particular friend. Nonetheless, focus on the consequences of a relationship itself might cause us to seek peers of convenience or transactional advantage. It is not in fact an invitation to a radical, gracious relationship, informed by the good news of God's new creation of his people as the body of Christ (1 Cor. 12:27), the temple of the Holy Spirit (1 Cor. 6:19). For such a relationship, we must look to virtue theory.

Virtue theory fits well with the idea of Christian discipleship. As Mark Mattes rightly notes, disciples no longer have to ask "'how am I saved?' but instead, 'what is my life about?'"[6] What kind of person do I want to be? Freed from worry about earning enough points to merit heaven, Christian friendship involves a shared mission to promote God's healing of the world as we join with friends in pursuit of goodness, truth, and beauty. This is the approach that best fits with perplexing times, times when it is hard to know how to act in a culture that's changing very quickly. Virtue ethics emphasizes the importance of being able to have the sort of internal character that can act heroically and with justice, not because of legalistic rules, or cold calculation, but because they have internalized noble values.

The formal conceptualization of virtue ethics began with Aristotle, in his *Nicomachean Ethics*. Training in virtue, of course, has a much more ancient history and often was taught through myths about virtuous heroes. In such narratives, it is rarely necessary to explain to audiences which of the characters are the "good guys" and which are the "bad guys." The stories themselves tend to make these judgments rather obvious. What Aristotle contributed, however, was an explanation of how virtue is identified, practiced, and protected.

Aristotle taught that virtue could be identified by finding a middle point between a vice of excess and a vice of defect: the so-called *golden mean*. The problem with virtue theory in the public square is often that philosophers do not always agree on how to determine or establish particular virtue. Christians, fortunately, have the advantage of being able to turn to the chief virtues of faith, hope, and love, which are clearly celebrated in biblical revelation. Regardless, Aristotle's golden mean can be helpful for clarifying practical aspects of friendship.[7] We will explore several particular virtues related to friendship below. In the meantime, I acknowledge that the general wisdom of following a middle way is not universally applicable. For instance, Christians don't seek moderation when it comes to the theological virtues of faith, hope, and love. These are infinite, given their divine source. Likewise, spiritual fruits like joy, grace, and peace (Gal. 5:22–23) have an inexhaustible source and ought to be poured out by God's people without reserve.

Aristotle taught that the virtues are best fostered in society through *habituation*. By practicing virtues, even when they don't come naturally, we begin to internalize virtue and pattern our lives accordingly. In a sense, we fake it till we make it. Friendship offers an opportunity for us to practice the virtues together. Friends encourage each other toward virtue and offer candid, constructive criticism when one or the other slides into patterns of vice. In a broader culture that constantly shapes us through patterns of life based on false values—what J. K. A. Smith describes as "secular liturgies"[8]—friends shaped by the logic of the Gospel provide each other with a "counter-formation," a new pattern of life, shaped by Christ's model. This isn't about mutual nagging but rather through joyful camaraderie as collaborators with God's redeeming mission in the world.

Aristotle taught that the virtues are best cultivated within a healthy *ethos*. An ethos is the culture of a community. This is where friendship becomes especially important. On the one hand, vicious ethos (and thus vicious friends) have a devastating negative affect on virtue: "Bad company corrupts good character" (1 Corinthians 15:33 NIV). Consider how this works in law enforcement, for example. A well-intentioned rookie cop might find it difficult to fulfill his or her calling with integrity if the rest of the department is crooked.[9] On the other hand, surrounded by the living communion of saints, those who are salt of the world (Matt. 5:13) and the good yeast that leavens the whole dough (Luke 13:20–21) draw from the support of the virtuous community as they encounter ever-new moral challenges of the contemporary world.

For Aristotle, the goal (Greek: *telos*) of all of this is clear: *happiness*. Fulfilling one's purpose (we might say *vocation*) along the lines of excellence is the essence of virtue. This sort of virtue, in the company of true friends, leads to contentment since one's life is filled with meaning and excellence. This meaning isn't about the aggrandizement of one's ego, but rather is about the joy of enjoying meaningful connections with other disciples and fellow wayfarers through this life.

The Golden Mean and Friendship

For Aristotle, friendship was either a virtue itself or at least something that involves virtue.[10] Moreover, its main purpose is to foster and provide a way of conveying virtue.[11] But how does one determine what a virtue is? Though clearly stated biblical virtues are usually easier to identify directly in Scripture, applying Aristotle's concept of the golden mean can often be an effective way of locating virtue and distinguishing its related vices. Aristotle's attention to the midpoint between excess and defect, however, can be helpful for clarifying the nature of virtue within friendship. It can also help us steer clear of common ways in which friendship can actually become problematic for the ethical life. Permit me to illustrate this with three virtues: fidelity, hospitality, and honesty. Consider the following table, which I took the liberty of creating, using Aristotle's concept of the golden mean:

Vice of Defect	Virtue	Vice of Excess
Fickleness	Fidelity	Cronyism and Conspiracy
Disregard	Hospitality	Codependency
Insincere Flattery	Honesty	Judgmentalism

(1) *Fidelity* or faithfulness is clearly a noble virtue in a friend. We sometimes think of this in terms of *loyalty*. This can generally be a fine way to think of it, so long as we include the possibility of being part of a "loyal opposition" when needed. Fickleness is a vice of defect because it represents a lack of reliable friendship. It stems from personal selfishness and dependence on transactional thinking in a relationship. Perhaps more problematic these days, however, is the vice of excess, in which we give unfair advantages to friends. This is especially problematic when we confuse fidelity to friends with covering over or ignoring abusive or corrupt behavior. As was painfully made clear with the Roman Catholic Church's handling of priestly sexual abuse scandals, choosing to protect and conceal the misdeeds of peers ultimately failed to truly help both the victims and the perpetrators. It allowed heinous deeds to go unaddressed, and the widespread negative effects of this approach are manifest.

Not all misdeeds of friends should be exposed, however. When a sin is committed against us, we are encouraged to avoid keeping a record of wrongs (1 Cor. 13:5). Forgiveness, after all, is central to the way of Jesus. This involves a radical invitation to a new logic of unconditional love. Christians also are to refrain from gossip, the highlighting of others' sins, often to make ourselves appear superior to others. There are thus times—understood in light of Christian freedom—when it is appropriate to cover over the sins of others. Eastern theologian Isaac the Syrian (613–700) reflects this thinking in the following provocative passage:

Let yourself be persecuted, but do not persecute others.

Be crucified, but do not crucify others.

Be slandered, but do not slander others.

Rejoice with those who rejoice, and weep with those who weep: such is the sign of purity.

Suffer with the sick.

Be afflicted with sinners.

Exult with those who repent.

Be the friend of all, but in your spirit remain alone.

Be a partaker of the sufferings of all, but keep your body distant from all.

Rebuke no one, revile no one, not even those who live very wickedly.

Spread your cloak over those who fall into sin, each and every one, and shield them. And if you cannot take the fault on yourself and accept punishment in their place, do not destroy their character.[12]

In this piece of radical Christian advice, notice that Isaac suggests we might even choose to take the consequences of sin upon ourselves. What none of this can overlook, however, are instances in which a friend presents an ongoing danger or negative consequence to *someone else*, especially when that someone is in a position of vulnerability. Churches and other organizations must be vigilant, placing the safety of children, women, and the oppressed far above our desire to help out our close associates and even our genuine friends. Perhaps, therefore, "reliability," "honesty," and "fidelity" are better concepts than "loyalty."

(2) *Hospitality* is a mark of Christian virtue for people in general, but the intimacy of friendship allows many opportunities for radical hospitality. Throughout my life, having friends who were willing to come through with assistance has been a priceless blessing. Likewise, I've experienced joy in sharing resources, providing space in my home, and helping friends' families out when they were in need. This mutual aid is a supreme benefit of friendship and an opportunity to reflect the selfless love of God toward others. Unfortunately, this virtue also sits between two potential vices.

Sometimes, when we are harried by the demands of life, we fail to hear the cries of friends (literal and figurative). We get so obsessed with our own egotistical desires that we disregard the needs and hurts of a friend. To remedy this, we can learn to be present when we are with friends. I must confess that this is particularly hard for me. I am easily distracted by nature and always busy with an array of projects, and I talk too much when there is an uncomfortable silence. I try to work on these negative characteristics daily, but it is hard to fight biology and lifelong behavioral patterns. Nonetheless, by being present and attuned to a friend, it is possible to begin to set aside resentment of the past and release anxiety about the future. This is spiritual wisdom for more than just friendship, and important to our own wellbeing, but it is particularly valuable and effective within a friendship.

Codependency resembles a vice of excess, an inauthentic exaggeration of hospitality. I'm using the term broadly here, and for more than unhealthy relationships that involve addiction. Codependency here can, for instance, describe a situation in which we are so worried about making sure we are liked by a friend that we fail to set appropriate boundaries. Desiring approval from and close connection to a friend—especially when we have a weak sense of self—we might find ourselves becoming emotionally drained by a needy friend. Moreover, we might inadvertently end up feeding a friend's unhealthy behavior by allowing them to avoid the implications of their addiction, behaviors, or state of mind. Christian freedom means that, while we never cease to love, there are times when it is appropriate and perhaps even a duty—for the sake of the friend—to withdraw somewhat. We can at least step back from behaviors or attitudes that foster a friend's unhealthy way of being.

(3) *Honesty* is perhaps the most valuable virtue for friendship. It is also the most difficult. It requires courage. It also requires a strong sense of self. Paradoxically, to be a true friend, we must be willing to lose that friendship for the sake of honest friendship. This doesn't mean we should share every opinion or disapproval, of course, but it does mean that we ought not hold back our candid beliefs and insights from friends.

It is relatively easy to see that false and insincere flattery is worthless. Nonetheless, flattery is rather common. When insincere, it stems from our personal insecurity. We want people to like us, because we think that determines whether *we* matter. Christians, however, having been baptized into Christ, have a new and secure identity. It is an eternal identity that has genuine meaning. With this knowledge, Christians need not worry about calling noble things noble, and bad acts bad. They are free to call things what they are, even if this offends a friend to do so. True friends will respect and learn to value this. False friends, or friends too personally insecure to receive genuine friendship, may withdraw. So be it.

Of course, we must be careful not to be overly confident when we speak our minds. We might, for instance, become legalistic and judgmental in our assessments. That would by no means be a mark of the gracious Christian community. We might also try to be slightly more sophisticated, like Job's friends, who tried to offer tough love and honest talk but didn't really know the whole story. We tend to have a bias toward a "just world" conception of existence. Such thinking involves something like the Hindu concept of karma—the idea that we get what we deserve and that there is an inevitable accounting for all deeds. But Christians recognize that, while we all are fallen, there are many evils that befall us not because of an exact karmic consequence but because the whole world is out of alignment due to collective sin. Our need to read the direct hand of God into our friends' calamities might make us feel better (so we can assume that as long as we keep our noses clean we won't have to experience tragedy), but it isn't a case of honesty.

Sometimes the most honest way to respond to a friend's misfortune is to admit that *we honestly don't understand what's going on.* This is the advice Dietrich Bonhoeffer gave in consideration of tragedy within our "penultimate" existence. The ultimate is God's final reality for creation. The penultimate is the second-to-last state of existence. It's the world in which we find ourselves right now. And this world is often one of mystery, inexplicable suffering, and uncertainty.

In line with Luther's understanding of the "already but not yet" reality of Christ's kingdom, Bonhoeffer suggests that Christians, encouraged by the ultimate promises in Scripture, may in many circumstances refrain from offering simplistic explanations of the suffering encountered by our friends. Instead, they might rightly choose to suffer alongside a friend, donning metaphorical sackcloth and ashes as a sign of sympathy as they grieve. In this, Christian friends serve as a witness to the eschatological promise that God's plan will ultimately prevail, even when we don't understand why suffering is occurring or how it will ultimately be redeemed. Bonhoeffer writes:

> [L]et us ask why it is that precisely in thoroughly grave situations, for
> instance when I am with someone who has suffered bereavement,
> I often decide to adopt a "penultimate" attitude, particularly when I
> am dealing with Christians, remaining silent as a sign that I shared
> in the bereaved person's helplessness in the face of such a grievous
> event, and not speaking the biblical words of comfort which are, in
> fact, known to me and available to me. Why am I unable to open my
> mouth, when I ought to give expression to the ultimate? And why,
> instead, do I decide on an expression of thoroughly human solidar-
> ity? Is it from mistrust of the power of the ultimate word? Is it from
> fear of people? Or is there some good positive reasons for such an
> attitude, namely, that my knowledge of the word, my having it at my
> fingertips, in other words my being, so to speak, spiritually master
> of the situation, bears only the appearance of the ultimate, but is in
> reality itself something entirely penultimate? Does not one in some
> cases, by remaining deliberately in the penultimate, perhaps point all
> the more genuinely to the ultimate, which God will speak in God's
> own time (though indeed even then through a human mouth)?[13]

In other words, Christians can let mysteries be mysteries not out of a
lack of trust, but because they rest securely in the ultimate goodness
and providence of God, the details of which we may be thoroughly
ignorant.

This business of the penultimate is typically appropriate for
moments of grief and trauma. Eventually, of course, there will be
appropriate opportunities to talk through the good that can come
out of what we learn from our suffering, and a good friend will
be thoughtful and sensitive about when those opportunities are at
hand. Usually, those opportunities have deep roots in the Gospel.
Furthermore, with a backdrop of God's grace, friends who can trust
one another can indeed move into an important function of honesty within friendship: safe and gracious vulnerability with a close
friend.

When friends can be thoroughly honest, they are genuine
friends indeed. They can give advice without worrying about how
it will affect the relationship. They can be honest about their own
failings. They can also be honest about their fears, doubts, and ideas.
And they can do this without having to worry about the negative
opinions of others. There have been few things more valuable in my

life than having a candid sounding board in the form of a true friend. There are few more precarious situations than when a person is too afraid to be honest with a confidant, since this can allow unhealthy thoughts and behaviors to fester.

Consider, for instance, one of many clergy scandals of recent memory. Megachurch pastor and president of the National Association of Evangelicals, Ted Haggard, fell from prominence in the wake of news he had been seeing a male prostitute who was also supplying him with methamphetamines. How did it get that far out of hand? There are many psychological and spiritual factors behind a person's misbehavior, but I am convinced things could have gone much differently for Haggard had he had the sort of friends with whom he could talk through his desires and addictions. He probably didn't have such people in his life because he thought he would never get a gracious hearing. And so, unaided by gracious friends, he fell deeper into risky and family-damaging behavior. Would not a modern Luther have been helpful by saying something like, "Sin boldly"? That is, not saying that he should sin more, or act on his worst impulses, but rather be open and honest about the sinful desires he detected in himself. I don't think such frank, grace-infused conversations would have encouraged Haggard to more misbehavior but instead to more appropriate counseling and self-awareness. There is value in private confession with a pastor. Many cases benefit greatly from clinical mental health care. Nevertheless, at the deepest level, a wise and sincere friend can be invaluable to one's growth and wellbeing.

Selecting and Maintaining Good Friends

If indeed friendship involves vulnerability, risk, and painful honesty, it is therefore wise to choose trustworthy friends. The Proverbs have a lot to say on this matter:

> One who is righteous [chooses his friends carefully],
>   but the way of the wicked leads them astray. (12:26)

> Whoever walks with the wise becomes wise,
>   but the companion of fools will suffer harm. (13:20)

> Make no friendship with a man given to anger,
>   nor go with a wrathful man,
> lest you learn his ways
>   and entangle yourself in a snare. (22:24–25)

Christian freedom means we are free to select and cultivate friendships that encourage wisdom, virtue, and a peaceful life.

The question then arises: How ought one select friends? Transactional advantage, as we've noted, isn't our primary criterion. This is reinforced by most classical moral teachers, whether Christian or pagan. Aristotle agreed that we form friendships because we care about what is noble in them and also taught that one should end a friendship when the friend gets caught up in vice but not before first trying to bring them back to virtue.[14] Jesus notes that even the wicked choose friends based on what they can get out of the relationship, but not because they admire each other (Matt. 5:46–47). For Christians, friendship isn't about what we get out of a relationship directly. We should especially avoid selecting friends who can feed our egos. For instance, we should not choose one friend over another because he or she is more successful in worldly terms, because his or her attractiveness might rub off on us, or because he or she has the reins of power. Often, Christians ought to befriend the beautiful losers, the outsiders, the downtrodden, and the foreigner. The process depends not on the old worldly logic of exchange but on the new Gospel-based logic of mutual gift giving. The most beautiful gift exchange between friends is the gift of mutual support and encouragement among comrades on the quest for the transcendental virtues, allies within God's mission of healing and reconciling the world to himself.

Augustine channels the idea of Platonic love, in which something noble in another person stirs us up toward contemplation of the ideals. For him,

> You only love your friend truly, after all, when you love God in your friend, either because he is in him, or in order that he may be in him. That is true love and respect. There is no true friendship unless You weld it between souls that cling together by the charity poured forth in their hearts by the Holy Spirit.[15]

To the extent that our friendships resemble Augustine's concept here, we will find that they guide us to a sense of God's reality, which aligns and empowers our ethical lives.

Can We Be Friends with People Who Hold Drastically Different Views on Life?

One potential pitfall of forms of friendship is that we have a lazy tendency to only keep friends who are similar to ourselves. This creates echo chambers where we may unwittingly reinforce the worst characteristics in our midst. Without getting outside our parochial circles, we sometimes fail to see how we are coming across to the larger world, and we also fail to understand what others outside are trying to say to us. I admit that I just spent a bunch of time explaining that we are free to choose friends as we find delight in them. I also said that it is good to choose friends who share similar values. If I'm at liberty to like people who like what I like, and value what I value, isn't that going to lead to a lack of difference in my group of friends? Sure, we're free to act that way. But it is as unwise as it is potentially boring.

Augustine's teaching on friendship involves frequent anxiety about the instability and uncertainty of friendship.[16] Indeed, those who read Augustine's *Confessions* probably can recall at least a few times in which his friends were bad news. There was a gang called the Wreckers, friends who convinced Augustine to go to the gladiatorial games despite his moral objections, and the famous incident when he and his pals stole pears, just because they could. It's no wonder then, why, though Augustine believed firmly in the importance of friendship, he also realized that a clique of friends could easily degenerate into a vicious mob.

When you hear the word *diversity*, what do you think and feel? Do you have an immediately negative reaction? If so, ask yourself, why? Ask yourself whether meeting more, different people might change your perspective on the word. Ask yourself whether it might not be your experience with different people that makes you uneasy. Perhaps you aren't ready to partake in this thought experiment, since all you can think of is a stereotype of nagging HR departments and bureaucratic, tokenistic diversity. Or perhaps you're a different sort of reader and love diversity like you love exotic cuisine. Or perhaps you believe that the essence of Jesus' message is that the gospel opens our spiritual family to men and women, the high and low born, and people from every nation. Whatever the case, please don't let your initial emotive response to "diversity" get in the way of diversifying your group of friends.

Maybe you can be persuaded by self-interest here. Diversity can be incredibly helpful, even to your worldly success. Diversify your portfolio, or you might end up overinvested in a soon-to-be-obsolete industry. Diversify your crops, or a pest swarm might wipe out your year's produce. Diversify your diet, or you might have too much of some chemicals and too few of important nutrients. Diversify your medical opinions, or you might miss an important treatment option. Solicit diverse insights from an executive team at work, and you'll be a better CEO. Why, then, would you want a boring existence only among virtual clones . . . of *you*?

Ethnic, gender,[17] and economic diversity is important with respect to friendship. Developing relationships that transcend these divisions, even when it doesn't change our minds or allegiances, at least makes us more understanding and thoughtful people. We at least understand why others see things in different ways. When friends with whom we disagree, about politics for instance, can still remain our friends, this helps us help each other hone our arguments and commitments. But these are only a few types of diversity. More importantly, diverse friends represent a helpful barometer of our actual breadth of experience. If we think we are open to learning from other people, but everyone looks like us, they might also think like us. Sure, they may be *other Baptists* or *other Democrats* or *other Broncos fans*, but your differences are probably a lot more in-house and connected than you realize. This is why we should seek diverse friendships for the same reason C.S. Lewis thought we should read old books. He writes:

> Every age has its own outlook. It is specially good at seeing certain truths and specially liable to make certain mistakes. We all, therefore, need the books that will correct the characteristic mistakes of our own period. And that means the old books. All contemporary writers share to some extent the contemporary outlook—even those, like myself, who seem most opposed to it. Nothing strikes me more when I read the controversies of past ages than the fact that both

sides were usually assuming without question a good deal which we should now absolutely deny. They thought that they were as completely opposed as two sides could be, but in fact they were all the time secretly united—united with each other and against earlier and later ages—by a great mass of common assumptions.[18]

Broadening our friendships, in a manner similar to this insight from Lewis, helps us to be properly critical of our common assumptions. But why does this matter? Is this sort of talk nothing but a politically correct shame game? No. I'm not inviting you to agree with me here so you don't get nagged, culturally shamed, or fired. Do it because it will bring you delight, gratitude, and growth. Do it to spread the love of Christ to someone you might not have ordinarily become acquainted with, and enjoy the little surprises that arise in your interactions. Echo chambers only reinforce our Old Adam—that is, our false, terribly contrived egos. But what of the idea that friends should share a commitment to the transcendentals—goodness, truth, and beauty—to a common mission? Ah, now we're at the real point! Friendship isn't about fitting in with a clique. It's about the mission. The true mission—the Way—dissolves my concern for whether someone is like me or not. This may take us on interesting journeys, with unlikely friends. For instance, if I want to understand what God wants for me in this life, I might do well to have a friend who adheres to a different religion. We share in this case a desire to know, love, and serve God. But who is God? We often disagree on that matter, of course. If, on the other hand, I meet someone who is a part of my own community, and worships in the same church, but ultimately has no real interest in understanding God or following his way of love in this world, that person is less likely to provide a good, close friendship. The key is that both friends must be interested in pursuing the good, true, and beautiful, not that they must see eye to eye on what these things are just yet.

Mimetic Desire, Violence, and Friendship

A final word of caution is in order, with respect to friendship. Remember the story of King Arthur, his pal Lancelot, and Guinevere? There is a reason why that love-triangle-inspired discord is so common in world narratives. Friends tend to mirror each other, especially their values, desires, and interests. When one of those interests is not in abundant supply—such as in the case of a single love interest—friends can find themselves in an unwanted struggle. This reality was at the heart of the philosophy of French intellectual René Girard (1923–2015).[19] I was fortunate to have been able to hear him firsthand in grad school. And while I recognize there are some helpful clarifications and counterpoints to his life's thesis,[20] I think his insights are important and insightful.

Here's my playful summary of how his concept plays out. Consider two buddies. They come from similar but distant rural towns and find themselves roommates at a state university. They become fast friends. By the end of the semester, they wear the same golf shirts. They both listen to Sublime. They both love roller hockey. They both get into mountain biking. They really dig hanging out, because they have so many shared values. Their desires become confused. Who was it that first got into ska? Which guy first bought a mountain bike off Craigslist?

And then, who was the first to have a crush on Alexis? That's the woman in their English class who fits *both* of their ideals. You see, their ideals have merged. And this was pleasant for a long while. But now, there is a limited resource. This causes conflict. One night, after playing beer pong, the two friends get into a fight about who should ask Alexis out. Fists start flying. Their friends intervene. They really enjoy each other's company. So, the only way for them to stay friends without (metaphorically) killing each other is to make Alexis a scapegoat.

"Yeah," says one, "we shouldn't be fighting over her. She's just a slut. She got in the way of our friendship."

The other nods in agreement: "Yeah: bros before hoes, man. Am I right?"[21] Thus, they (metaphorically) kill Alexis to get her out of the way and restore balance.[22]

For Girard, this conflict is an ancient, profound, and pervasive one. This pattern of similar values is what he calls "mimetic desire." He believes that this process of *scapegoating* (what happened to Alexis in my illustration above) is the reason why the idea of sacrifice is at the bedrock of human culture. The ritual violence and inner fighting of communities is so pervasive that, according to Girard, it is why the final command(s) to not *covet* is far more important and fundamental to our human condition than we often realize. He writes:

> The tenth and last commandment is distinguished from those preceding it both by its length and its object: in place of prohibiting an act it forbids a desire (Exod. 20:17). . . . The desire prohibited by the tenth commandment must be the desire of all human beings—in other words, simply desire as such. . . . If this desire is the most common of all, what would happen if it were permitted rather than forbidden? There would be perpetual war in the midst of all human groups, subgroups, and families. . . . If individuals are naturally inclined to desire what their neighbors possess, or to desire what their neighbors even simply desire, this means that rivalry exists at the very heart of human social relations. This rivalry, if not thwarted, would permanently endanger the harmony and even the survival of all human communities. . . . The commandment that prohibits desiring the goods of one's neighbor attempts to resolve the number one problem of every human community: internal violence.[23]

What's the solution to all this? We must kill not our friend, or what we desire, but our Old Adam, our false egos. Only then can a friendship be safe, stable, and free from such conflict. Our Old Adam loves to possess things. It does not so much relate to people as it uses them to accessorize the façade of its own identity. A friend makes the Old Adam look good when the friend is successful and attractive. The Old Adam likes to assemble lots of shallow but advantageous allies. It seeks a "trophy" spouse—one who will reward their sense of importance, power, and worthiness. But when a person is to spiritually drown the Old Adam in baptism, *and also in their thinking*, they don't have to fret when friends succeed, do well, or fall in love. They have released their desire to hoard the world. They are meek and spiritually poor. And because of that, they get the whole world back. They don't have to cling too tightly, and so they rest easy in friendship and in romance. The point of all of this is that a shaky sense of self, a glory-starved ego—our rascally Old Adam—will get in the way of our ability to rest easy in friendship. Through Christ, we have the infinite. So there is, in the end, no reason to hoard things, people, and decorations for our ego.

Friendship as Antidote to Existential Despair and Loneliness

To bring things to a close, permit me to suggest what I think is the most valuable aspect of friendship: it is an antidote to existential despair and loneliness. This has ethical implications, because without spiritual peace and a sense of ultimate hope, it is incredibly difficult to care much at all about doing good in the world. This loss of hope is called *sloth*. The vice of sloth is often misunderstood. Most assume it's another word for laziness. But sloth is about a lack of hope. When one loses hope, this is called despair. It is can take the form of an overwhelming loneliness. This leads to despondency. A slothful person is inactive not because of low physical energy but because he or she lacks a passion for life, an awareness of the fact that life is a blessing and a gift. Trapped in our unhealthy mental loops, fixating on resentment, fear, and anxiety, we withdraw into loneliness. This turning in on ourselves is how Luther describes sin in general: the great tragedy of sin is that we are curved in on ourselves (*incurvatus in se*), as opposed to focusing our gaze outward onto Christ, and subsequently focusing outward toward others, as faithful masks of God (*larvae Dei*).

Friendship's key vocation just might be mutual encouragement in hope against the despair of existential loneliness. Incidentally, this is why dogs are popular. They are "man's best friend" because they have a way of keeping people from turning in on themselves, especially when they live alone. As nice as pups are, the great value of a human friend is that they can be the face of God and, more to the point, the *mouthpiece of God*, reminding us that God has everything under control, that all manner of thing shall be well. That we have forgiveness. That we are loved. Whenever we cry out something like "*Eli Eli lama sabachthani?*" (Eccles. 4:9–10), when we feel that God has left us and is nowhere to be seen, we are reminded of the grace and presence of God, in the presence of a friend. Not everyone has that blessing. So, whenever we can, we do well to reach out and be a friend to those who might feel abandoned. This is not a burden but a delight. As Augustine said, "What better consolation is there in this mortal world than the sincere loyalty and mutual love of good and genuine friends."[24]

Recap

We've covered a lot of territory. First, I argued that virtue theory is the best approach to the ethical issues related to friendship. Next, I examined the virtues of fidelity, hospitality, and honesty (along with their related vices of excess and defect) to show how friendship can go wrong when unbalanced. Then, I showed that though friendship is nontransactional, it is nevertheless selective, based on a shared mission. Despite the importance of commonality, I also argued that it is important to diversify friends to avoid echo chambers that can breed misunderstanding and vice. Then I took us on an exploration deeper into the darkness, where we saw that shared values and desires between friends can lead to violence if individual friends do not "drown the Old Adam" by letting go of their false egos. Finally, despite these dangers, I contended that friends help us combat despair and loneliness by reminding us we are loved and forgiven. This allows us to be faithful masks of God in the world, since we are freed from worrying about adding to our own sense of self, and turn outward to the other, equipped with the unconditional love of God.

Luther and Melanchthon

A Reformation Friendship

Scott L. Keith, PhD, and Caleb E. Keith

> I prefer the books of Master Philip [Melanchthon] to my own. I am rough, stormy, and altogether warlike. I am here to fight innumerable monsters and devils. I must remove all stumps and stones, cut away thistles and thorns, and clear the wild forests, but Master Philip comes along softly and gently, sowing and watering with joy, according to the gifts which God has abundantly bestowed upon him.[1]

It is hard to imagine what the Reformation would have looked like without the cooperative effort of Martin Luther and Philip Melanchthon. At the heart of this cooperation is the fact that these two men were drastically different. Robert Kolb calls Luther "a preacher, proclaiming God's love and his demands directly to his people from the pulpit." Melanchthon, on the other hand, was "a teacher concerned to explain ideas and the connections between ideas to students."[2] These differences show up in their academic backgrounds, styles of writing, and personalities. However numerous their differences, we can observe and study them in unison because of how united they stood on the doctrine of justification and its recovery in the church. It was Christ crucified for the forgiveness of sin that drew them together, and it was that forgiveness declared to one another that kept them together. Thus, the relation between Luther and Melanchthon can really only be characterized as a friendship.

Getting to Know One Another

To best understand the friendship of Luther and Melanchthon, we must first grasp the similarities and differences of their vocations. This is important first because Luther and Melanchthon were both called to Wittenberg to teach. Luther was called as a zealous monk to teach biblical theology at the University of Wittenberg in 1511. Luther had been in the monastery for six years before receiving his professorship, and it would be another six years before his famous Ninety-five Theses would be nailed to the Castle Church door. In contrast, Melanchthon arrived in Wittenberg not as a professor of theology but of Greek in 1518. His arrival was in the midst of Luther's early reformational debates, including the disputations at Heidelberg and the debate against John Eck. At Wittenberg, Luther started a theological war into which a young Melanchthon was quickly drafted and then, whether he liked it or not, elevated to general.

At the university, and when it came to the theological debate at large, there always stood an unavoidable age and rank difference between Luther and Melanchthon. Luther was fourteen years Melanchthon's senior. He was not just a professor but a doctor of theology, and he served as chair of the theology department. These differences were in no way negative but rather shaped the scope of their friendship.

When Philp Melanchthon was first called to teach at the University of Wittenberg, he was called to be professor of Greek grammar. He was young, very young by today's standards, only twenty-one years of age. He was already known as a great Humanist scholar, second only to the great Erasmus of Rotterdam. Both Melanchthon and Erasmus were early on intrigued by Luther's teachings. Yet, unlike Erasmus, when Melanchthon was called to Wittenberg, he was brought under Luther's protective and instructive wing.

Eventually, Melanchthon found that he agreed with Luther, especially Luther's analysis of St. Paul's epistles.[3] Luther found that this *young grammarian* had an intriguing and keen intellect. Luther would often sit in on Melanchthon's lectures as his young protégé lectured in Greek on the gospel of John and Paul's letter to the church in Rome. When students published these lectures without Melanchthon's knowledge or permission, they did so with Luther's direct encouragement. Through this direct mentorship, somewhat coy approach to encouragement, and mutual admiration, a friendship began that would last twenty-eight years, until Luther's death in 1546.

It is true, then, that as soon as Melanchthon arrived in Wittenberg, his very close collaboration with Luther began. Luther improved his Greek with Melanchthon's help. Melanchthon started a regular study of theology and became a determined follower of Luther. Years later, in his Testament of 1539, Melanchthon confessed with gratitude, "I learned the Gospel from him."[4] Just two years after their meeting, Melanchthon said, "he would rather die than be separated from Luther," and later that same year he stated, "Martin's welfare is dearer to me than my own life."[5]

My Father Teacher, Dr. Luther

Wilhelm Pauck notes, "Melanchthon revered Luther as his fatherly friend. In almost all his letters, he addressed him as *pater Carissimus*."[6] Likewise, Luther regularly boasted about Melanchthon and his work like a father might proudly brag about his son to family and friends. While he knew Melanchthon's strengths, he also knew his weaknesses. Melanchthon, by Luther's accounts, was plagued by anxiety. In 1530, while corresponding over the content and delivery of the *Augsburg Confession,* Luther wrote to Melanchthon, "Why then are you constantly tormenting yourself?" He went on, "I too am sometimes downcast, but not all the time. It is your philosophy that is tormenting you, not your theology, and the same is true of your friend Joachim, who seems to be troubled by similar anxiety."[7] The philosophy, which Luther later identified, was Melanchthon's desire to know or predict the outcomes of his work rather than simply resting in that what he wrote was biblical and true. In this struggle, Luther's constant strategy was to turn Melanchthon away from his thoughts of what might happen and instead preach that which was sure and had already happened at the cross of Christ.

The father and son distinction reminds us of the importance of vocation to ask, in what way is a father called to be a friend to his children that differs from how two young men of the same stature and position might serve as friends to one another? Melanchthon did not need a yes-man constantly telling him that his theological conclusions were right. Instead, he needed a father to tell him to stop worrying about his homework and just turn it in already. For what great gifts Melanchthon had intellectually, it seemed that he lacked a certain confidence to face rejection. What Melanchthon lacked in this area Luther made up for in spades, lending his confidence in the Gospel to Melanchthon at every opportunity. And while Luther identified, or at the least theorized, that philosophical categories were undermining Melanchthon's confidence, he did not oppose but rather encouraged him to use his Humanistic education in the service of the Gospel.

While they were both focused on the same goal, Luther and Melanchthon had different approaches and different personalities. Luther, even by self-description, was bold and outspoken while Melanchthon was quieter and more careful with his words. Both men struggled with depression, yet they dealt with their struggles in dramatically different ways. Luther, when depressed, would surround himself with family and friends, drowning his sorrows with a pint of his wife's carefully brewed beer. Melanchthon, when feeling the approach of his often-battled melancholy, would retreat to the library and attempt to find solace in the company of his books, where he would consult his long-dead friends, Aristotle, Quintilian, and Cicero.

Luther seems to have reveled in the inevitable controversies the Reformation stirred, while Melanchthon seems to be a reluctant soldier in the battle. Melanchthon once wrote to his good friend and eventual biographer: "If I were my own master, I would prefer to hide myself away in some kind of solitude than to be involved in such a throng of affairs,"[8] In the same letter, Melanchthon confesses: "I have been like Prometheus on the rock, I feel as if I must sink and die."[9]

The fatherly relationship revealed itself clearly during one of Melanchthon's bouts with depression. Melanchthon was notorious for not taking care of himself in times of need. This was true, too, of the times when he was battling the demons of his depression. His retreat into the solitude of his books at these times was not always good for his overall health and wellbeing. At one critical point, Melanchthon's mood led to a decline in his health so grievous that he could not get out of bed and seemed to be suffering from a fever. When Luther found out, he burst into the room where Melanchthon lie, finding his good friend and colleague, "deathly ill, changed beyond recognition, unable to hear or speak."[10] Luther went to the window and cursed at God, demanding that he hear his demand and heal his friend. Threatening God, Luther yelled, "if you want me to trust any of your other promises, you will heal my friend now."[11] Turning to Melanchthon, he demanded, "eat." When Melanchthon refused Luther threatened, "either eat or I will excommunicate you."

The Student Becomes the Teacher

Luther benefited greatly from Melanchthon's grammatical and dialectic skill. There is a stark contrast between the way in which Luther referred to his own written works. Pauck explains, "he tended to entertain a low opinion of his books and the products of his pen. With few exceptions, they seemed to him to be nothing but occasional writings which deserved to be forgotten."[12] But his estimation of the value of Melanchthon's work was quite the opposite. He described Melanchthon's work on the *Augsburg Confession* and the *Loci Communes* as gifts to the whole church that ought to be read and studied by all theologians.[13] This returns us to Kolb's "preacher and teacher" distinction. The occasional nature of Luther's library emphasizes his gift for getting to the bottom of a person's worries and concerns and directly applying the forgiveness and comfort of Christ. As one could imagine, the lasting struggles of the Reformation had a widespread effect. It is no small thing that Luther was able to speak so directly to both princes and shoemakers concerning the heart of their troubles. We must understand that Melanchthon's gift for doctrinal order and education was also a matter of comfort.

Luther often praised Melanchthon's skill at writing, emphasizing his apparent brevity. In 1585 after the death of both Luther and Melanchthon, David Chytraeus noted that Luther had even called Melanchthon his *praeceptor* or teacher.[14] The ability to clearly communicate doctrine in a generally accessible way helped put Luther's and others' minds to rest. In fact, Luther described

Melanchthon's first edition of his systematic theology, the *Loci Communes Theologici,* as so good and so informative that it ought to be canonized.[15] Melanchthon was poised and eager to reestablish the Christian intellectual heritage in the context of the Humanist and evangelical tradition. For this reason, he feared war more than Luther. Melanchthon believed war would lead to total loss of the Latin-Christian heritage and order. He wanted to see this tradition first reformed by the Gospel of Christ and second preserved for the furtherance of Christian education that the truth of the Gospel would not again become hidden.

Early on, Melanchthon's ability with languages also proved to be of great value to Luther. As mentioned above, not long after his arrival in Wittenberg, Melanchthon began to teach Luther Greek. This instruction was to have far-reaching consequences, for it brought Luther clarity concerning the faith. Luther had been planning to prepare his *Lectures on Galatians* (1516–1517) for publication. However, at the end of 1518 he destroyed the manuscript and started over; the new result was the *Shorter Commentary on Galatians* of 1519. In this commentary, which was ready for the printer in May, Luther made an interesting remark about his relationship with his young friend and colleague. There, Luther candidly said that it was Melanchthon who led him to clarity on the meaning of Hebrews 11:1, that meaning of faith that for so long had been an obstacle for him. Luther wrote: "I held tenaciously to the authority of Jerome on this doctrine . . . But since then I have begun to employ Philip Melanchthon as my teacher in Greek—a man young in respect to his body, but a hoary-headed sage in regard to his intellectual powers!—who would not let me understand it thus and showed me that *substantia* means 'faculties.'"[16] In other words, according to this definition, Luther now saw faith as a God-given gift that is made part of the believer, not something the believer contributes to the process of salvation. His "teacher in Greek" and friend had thus changed the course of Luther's teaching and the Reformation.

This working together in the languages of the Bible, Hebrew and Greek, also strengthened their friendship and the cause of the Reformation. When Luther sat to translate the Bible into German, Melanchthon was more often than not right by his side. This collaboration on translating and revising the Bible stretched over their

entire lives. Indeed, this relationship had a strong emotional component and for years continued to strengthen their friendship.[17]

Vocation and Friendship

While vocation helps define the uniqueness of Luther and
Melanchthon, it is at the same time the unifying force behind their
friendship. In their various capacities, they were both called to proclaim the Gospel of Christ. While at times that proclamation was to a
broad audience spanning the entire Western world, it was more often
to one another. In 1530 Luther used the phrase, "I a sinner, commend
you, a sinner," and others like it when writing back and forth with
Melanchthon. This mutual recognition of their sin is immediately
met with the reality that on account of Christ, such sin is no longer
held against them. Their friendship was not one of mutual interest.
Rather, it was one of mutual need for forgiveness. In other words, it
was a law and Gospel friendship. Not only were they both in need of
such forgiveness, but they also firmly believed that in every work the
other maintained the justification won by Christ as central.

Luther and Melanchthon were many things to one
another—colleagues, teachers, and mentors. However, what is clear
is that, more than these, they were friends. Their friendship was
resilient, beginning in the early stages of turmoil brought on by
the Reformation and ending only with death. This lasting friendship was not built upon constant exercises of strength but on the
regular confession of weakness and the need for strength from
the other man. Luther's boisterous confidence often rested on the
quiet Melanchthon, while Melanchthon's timid intellectualism
depended on Luther's confidence to be heard. The way they gave to
each other freely serves as a picture of what the freedom God gives
us in Christ looks like in daily life. Their friendship, in this sense, is
between "a sinner to a sinner." Despite all their rank and file differences, they were equals on this point. They were equals in Christ,
justified by his blood and made alive to live freely side by side, proclaiming their freedom to the world around them.

The Inklings

Friendship and Writing

Samuel P. Schuldheisz, MDiv

> Lo! We have heard in old days of the wisdom of the cunning-minded Inklings; how those wise ones sat together in their deliberations, skillfully reciting learning and song-craft, earnestly meditating. That was true joy![1]
>
> —J.R.R. Tolkien

Throughout history, certain places and people become so entwined together that they take on a life of their own. For theologians of the Reformation, there are Wittenberg and Martin Luther. For students of US history, there are Plymouth Rock and the Pilgrims. For readers and writers, there are Oxford and the Inklings.

The Inklings began to meet regularly in the early 1930s until their last meeting in October of 1949. Though relatively unknown at the time, the Inklings have now become synonymous with story-telling and scholarship, wit and wisdom, creativity and community. The Inklings centered around the friendship of C.S. Lewis and J.R.R. Tolkien. Several years after they first met, Lewis and Tolkien's circle of friends expanded to include other like-minded writers:

Owen Barfield, Hugo Dyson, Neville Coghill, Warren Lewis, Charles Williams, and Adam Fox, just to name a few.[2]

When Lewis invited Charles Williams, a writer and editor at Oxford University Press, to visit one of their regular gatherings, he described the Inklings as "a sort of informal club called the Inklings: the qualifications (as they have informally evolved) are a tendency to write, and Christianity." Some thirty years later, Tolkien gave a brief account of the Inklings, describing them as an "undetermined and unelected circle of friends who gathered about C.S.L. [Lewis], and met in his rooms in Magdalen . . . our habit was to read aloud compositions of various kinds (and lengths)."[3] Together, the Inklings shared a love of words, myth, and intellectual swordplay. Owing in part to the nature of this group of friends, the books, essays, and writings of this unique and unlikely literary band of brothers is prolific. By 1940, Lewis, Tolkien, and Williams had produced nearly forty books, essays, or articles between them.[4]

What began as a gathering of friends continues to captivate the friendships, faith, and imaginations of their contemporary admirers. Diana Pavlac Glyer observes, "The Inklings have been called the 20th century's most influential group of writers."[5] Similarly, C.S. Lewis's biographer, Alister McGrath, descriptively points to the Inklings meetings as "a crucible of literary creativity and energy."[6] Likewise, Colin Duriez characterizes them as "a little like the church; in existence where two or three gathered."[7] Above all, however, the Inklings were friends. This group of friends grew and revolved around the friendship of Tolkien and Lewis. Through his friendship with Owen Barfield, Hugo Dyson, and J.R.R. Tolkien, Lewis was brought back to the Christian faith. Friendship influenced their life and literary work from Oxford to Cambridge. And it was friendship that began the Inklings.

An Unexpected Friendship

Like a good book, friends must have something to bind them together, a mutual love, similar values, or a shared worldview. "Friendship," writes Lewis, "must be about something, even if it were only an enthusiasm for dominoes or white mice. Those who have nothing can share nothing; those who are going nowhere have no fellow travelers."⁸ The Inklings were fellow travelers, journeying together on the road of literature, imagination, and their shared Christian faith. The Inklings began, as many things do, with a common interest among friends. Individuals become fellow travelers and friends in that moment when they discover that they had something, or many things, in common, as Lewis writes in *The Four Loves*, "What? You too? I thought I was the only one."⁹

Ironically, though, when Lewis and Tolkien first met at an afternoon tea of Oxford professors in 1926, they had very little in common with each other. Tolkien was a devout Roman Catholic. Lewis was an atheist, though by this time he had begun to question many of his atheistic and philosophical assumptions. Tolkien held the Chair of Old English Literature (Anglo-Saxon) at Oxford. Not surprisingly, he firmly believed that the ancient languages (i.e., Old and Middle English), along with medieval texts such as *Beowulf*, should be the bedrock of any serious study of English. Lewis, on the other hand, was still a modernist at the time, and had not yet been cured of what he called his "chronological snobbery." He was firmly entrenched on the other side of Oxford's long-standing language and literature debate, grounding the study of English in modern literature. In general, this included literature written after Geoffrey Chaucer and his *Canterbury Tales* in the fifteenth century. When Lewis wrote about his first meeting with Tolkien in his diary, he quipped, "He is a smooth, pale, fluent little chap . . . no harm in him: he only needs a smack or so."¹⁰

All of this changed, however, as Tolkien and Lewis grew closer to one another. As their friendship grew, so did their mutual trust. Eventually, Tolkien won Lewis over to his side in the language and literature debate, and they became close allies and advocates for a reformed English syllabus at Oxford, which was accepted in 1931.

Not long after their first meeting, Lewis discovered that Tolkien gathered with a small group, known as the Coalbiters, to study Norse mythology in its original Icelandic. Old Norse mythology had long been one of Lewis's great literary loves. He was captivated by the "Northernness" he saw in it. It was also Norse mythology that gave Lewis his first encounter with joy, a dominant theme throughout his life and writing.

In 1929, their friendship grew deeper when Tolkien asked Lewis to read one of his own private poems that had been a work in progress. The poem was *The Lay of Leithian*, which later became part of his imaginative literary world of Middle-earth. Lewis was enthralled by the poem and remained one of the strongest supporters of Tolkien's writing.

Lewis and Tolkien found in each other fellow travelers with whom they could share their love of myth, stories, and creative writing. This further deepened their friendship with each other. As Lewis would later write in *The Four Loves*, "It is then that Friendship is born. And instantly they stand together in an immense solitude."[11] Earlier in *The Four Loves*, Lewis observes that, "Lovers are always talking to one another about their love; Friends hardly ever talk about their Friendship. Lovers are normally face to face, absorbed in each other; Friends, side by side, absorbed in some common interest."[12]

Thankfully, Lewis and Tolkien did occasionally write or talk about their friendship and their common interests. Their words give us a glimpse into the depth of their friendship. Lewis provided Tollers, as he affectionately called him, with enthusiastic support, constant encouragement, and a ready ear. Were it not for his friendship with Lewis, Tolkien's epic stories from his imaginative world of Middle-earth would have never been published.

> The unpayable debt that I owe to him is not 'influence' as it is ordinarily understood, but sheer encouragement. He was for long my only audience. Only from him did I ever get the idea that my 'stuff' could be more than a private hobby. But for his interest and unceasing eagerness for more I should never have brought The L[ord] of the R[ings] to a conclusion.[13]

Tolkien greatly influenced his friend Lewis as well. Tolkien taught Lewis the seminal connection between myth and fact, which Tolkien said goes to the heart of the Gospel. The Gospel, Tolkien taught Lewis, has all the elements of a good story yet with one important addition: it is the one true myth. Tolkien also helped Lewis understand what he had glimpsed many years earlier while reading George MacDonald's *Phantastes*: that good stories give us a joy beyond this world and a glimpse of the otherworldly in our own world. The reason for this, Tolkien wrote, is that man is a subcreator. We tell stories because God himself is the chief storyteller. We make music, art, and literature because we are God's creatures, made in his image.

The Fellowship of Friends

Lewis and Tolkien's friendship continued until Lewis's death in 1963. Even later in life, though their friendship cooled, there was always a deep respect and dear love of friends between them. And though we think of Lewis and Tolkien as the two towers of the Inklings, they did not stand alone. Tolkien and Lewis, writes Alister McGrath, grew in their friendship with one another and the Inklings, "through books, through friends, and through friends discussing books."[14] This community of writers and friends were as joyful, witty, and mysterious as their name, which Tolkien described as "a pleasantly ingenious pun in its way, suggesting people with vague or half-informed intimations and ideas plus those who dabble in ink."[15]

The Inklings met in Lewis's rooms at Magdalen College, Oxford, on Thursday evenings for tea, drinks, cigars, and literary critique of works in progress. In good hobbit fashion, they also met at the Eagle and Child every Tuesday for food and conversation. Commenting on these and similar gatherings, Lewis writes, "My happiest hours are spent with three or four old friends in old clothes tramping together and putting up in small pubs—or else sitting up till the small hours in someone's college rooms talking nonsense, poetry, theology, metaphysics over beer, tea and pipes."[16]

Tolkien, Lewis, and the Inklings shared many things. And like any good friends, they also had their share of differences. They frequently challenged one another in their public and private gatherings. Warren Lewis recounts in his memoirs that "to read to the Inklings was a formidable ordeal."[17] Hugo Dyson did not like *The Lord of the Rings*. Tolkien also disliked many of Lewis's religious writings, since he was neither a trained theologian nor a clergyman. Several years earlier, from 1927 to 1929, C.S. Lewis and his friend Owen Barfield exchanged a long series of letters known as the "Great War." In this battle of ideas, Barfield led Lewis to finally abandon his chronological snobbery, reevaluate his position on the New Testament, and consider more closely the relationship between language, metaphor, and myth.

While the Inklings were friends, some closer to each other than others, they were no collection of paper dolls. Their similar interests helped to form the bonds of friendship, while their differences, in the form of constructive critiques and disagreements, helped to strengthen those bonds. In *The Company They Keep,* Diana Pavlac Glyer offers a well-balanced view of the Inklings, recognizing their similarities and differences that strengthened this circle of friends and their common interests with each other. "The Inklings shared a passionate concern for a rather unusual constellation of interests: Christianity, myth, imaginative literature, linguistics, and history. However, within each of these interests, they held very different points of view . . . a diversity of perspectives within a unity of interests—provides a clearer picture of the nature of the Inklings."[18]

Like two blades of a good pair of scissors, the Inklings' differences often helped to sharpen their work and strengthen their friendship. These friendships, in turn, spilled over into every facet of life, but especially their writing. As friends and writers, they functioned as "resonators, opponents, editors, and collaborators" presenting, critiquing, and reading various works of poetry, history, or stories.[19]

The close friendships of Lewis, Tolkien, and the Inklings is further revealed by the dedications in several of their books. C.S. Lewis dedicated the first book in his space trilogy, *Out of the Silent Planet,* to his brother, Warren, and later dedicated *The Screwtape Letters* to Tolkien. Lewis also dedicated his book *The Problem of Pain* to the Inklings, as did Tolkien in the first edition of *The Lord of the Rings.*

Friendship is a dominant and recurring theme in the Inklings' literary worlds as well. In Lewis's Space Trilogy, the main character, Elwin Ransom, bears several similarities to his friend Tolkien. Ransom, like Tolkien, is a professor and a philologist. Even Ransom's first name, Elwin, draws upon the Old English word *Ælfwine,* meaning elf friend. Tolkien, likewise, refers to Lewis in *The Lord of the Rings,* giving his character Treebeard some of Lewis's distinctive personality. The great Ent Treebeard and his famous cadence *"Hrum Hroom is an attempt to capture the booming voice of C.S. Lewis."*[20]

For the Inklings, good friends and good books went hand in hand. Like good books, good friends enrich and enliven the ordinary things in daily life. They give us joy and point us to what is true, good, and beautiful. And some of the best friends, and stories will point us to Jesus, the friend of sinners. On Saturday night, September 19 and into the early morning of September 20, 1931, two of Lewis's friends, J.R.R. Tolkien and Hugo Dyson, did exactly that.

Friendship, Faith, Myth, and Fact

The Inklings began with friendship. Friendship filled and fueled their writings. And it was through friendship that Lewis was brought back to the Christian faith. His longtime friend Arthur Greeves and his "Great War" over language and meaning with Owen Barfield all played an essential role in Lewis's journey back to Christianity. However, it was Tolkien and Dyson's nighttime conversation with Lewis that was instrumental in removing Lewis's final roadblocks on his pilgrim's regress back to Christianity. Since 1930, Lewis had believed in God, though he could not understand "how the life and death of Jesus Christ 2000 years ago could help us here and now." In their discussion on myth and metaphor that September night along Addison's Walk, beside Oxford's River Cherwell, Tolkien and Dyson helped Lewis understand that Christianity was both true and meaningful. "Tolkien helped Lewis to realise [sic] that a 'rational faith' was not necessarily emotionally barren. When rightly understood, the Christian faith could integrate reason, longing, and imagination."[21]

With Tolkien's guidance, Lewis came to see reason and imagination not as contradictory, but as compatible and complementary. The intellect and imagination are God's gifts, and both are present in the one great story of Christianity—the birth, life, death, and resurrection of Jesus. When Lewis recounted this nighttime conversation with his friend Arthur Greeves, he summarized it this way: "Now the story of Christ is simply a true myth: a myth working on us in the same way as the others, but with this tremendous difference that it really happened."[22] The joy Lewis had felt for so long, he had finally found in Christ. As St. Augustine had discovered centuries ago, Lewis's heart, imagination, and intellect were no longer restless, for he had found his rest in Christ's promises. Lewis's imagination and intellect quickly became focused on Christianity, side by side throughout the rest of his life, just like good friends.

In a letter to his friend Dom Bede Griffiths in 1941, Lewis recalled his friendship with Tolkien and the Inklings: "What I owe to them is incalculable. Dyson and Tolkien were the immediate human causes of my own conversion. Is any pleasure on earth as great as a circle of Christian friends by a good fire?"[23] Lewis no doubt had his friendship with Tolkien and the other Inklings in mind when he wrote this famous passage in *The Four Loves*.

> Those are the golden sessions; when four or five of us after a hard day's walking have come to our inn; when our slippers are on, our feet spread out towards the blaze and our drinks at our elbows; when the whole world, and something beyond the world, opens itself to our minds as we talk; and no one has any claim on or any responsibility for another, but all are freemen and equals as if we had first met an hour ago, while at the same time an Affection mellowed by the years enfolds us. Life—natural life—has no better gift to give. Who could have deserved it?[24]

For Lewis, friendship was a divine gift, evidence of God's undeserved grace. For in the love of a good friend, we can see the love of Christ. In his friendship with Lewis, Tolkien lived up to his name Reuel, friend of God. Tolkien pointed his friend Lewis to the love of God in Christ, the friend of sinners. And in Lewis, Tolkien found steadfast support, encouragement, and a friend with whom he could share his love of myth. Through the dark days of war, disease, and death, they dabbled in ink together as fellow travelers and friends. Their friendship with each other, and the other Inklings, enriched their lives, encouraged their writing, and inspired their imagination. They were friends who wrote, and they wrote about friendship.

Tolkien and Lewis also brought the gift of friendship to life within their literary and imaginative worlds. Along with their fellow Inklings, they believed that the best stories shed light on life in this world and reflect the light of another world, a light no darkness can overcome. They were fellow pilgrims on their journey to their true home. In Middle-earth, it was known as the Undying Lands to the West. In Narnia, it was known as Aslan's Country in the East. In Christianity, they discovered joy, friendship, and an answer to their longing in the greatest story of all, the Gospel of Jesus Christ.

For Tolkien and Lewis, the story of Christianity is the greatest story because it is both meaningful and true, beautiful and factual, captivating both our intellect and imagination. Tolkien said it best:

> The Gospels contain a fairy story, or a story of a larger kind which embraces all the essence of fairy-stories. They contain many marvels—peculiarly artistic, beautiful, and moving: "mythical" in their perfect, self-contained significance; and among the marvels is the greatest and most complete conceivable eucatastrophe. But this story has entered History and the primary world; the desire and aspiration of sub-creation has been raised to the fulfillment of Creation. The Birth of Christ is the eucatastrophe of Man's history. The Resurrection is the eucatastrophe of the story of the Incarnation. This story begins and ends in joy. It has pre-eminently the "inner consistency of reality." There is no tale ever told that men would rather find was true, and none which so many skeptical men have accepted as true on its own merits.[25]

Appendix A: A Selected Inklings Bibliography

- *Poetic Diction: A Study in Meaning*—Owen Barfield
- *The Silver Trumpet*—Owen Barfield
- *Poets and Storytellers: A Book of Critical Essays*—Lord David Cecil
- Nevill Coghill's translation of *The Canterbury Tales* (1951)
- *The Collected Papers of Nevill Coghill*—ed. Douglas Gray
- *Remembering C.S. Lewis: Recollections of Those Who Knew Him*—James Dundas Grant, ed. James T. Como
- *Old King Coel: A Rhymed Tale in Four Books*—Adam Fox
- *The Chronicles of Narnia*—C.S. Lewis
- *The Space Trilogy*—C.S. Lewis
- *The Four Loves*—C.S. Lewis
- *Mere Christianity*—C.S. Lewis
- *The Screwtape Letters*—C.S. Lewis
- *The Problem of Pain*—C.S. Lewis
- *Essays Presented to Charles Williams*
- *The Splendid Century*—W.H. Lewis
- *Memoir of C.S. Lewis*—W.H. Lewis

- *The Silmarillion*—though written by J.R.R. Tolkien, Christopher was finally able to publish his father's beloved book in 1977.
- *The History of Middle-earth*—Christopher Tolkien
- *Unfinished Tales of Numenor and Middle-earth*—further work of Tolkien published posthumously by his son, Christopher.
- *The Monster and the Critics and Other Essays*—ed. Christopher Tolkien
- *The Hobbit*—J.R.R. Tolkien
- *The Letters of Father Christmas*—J.R.R. Tolkien
- *The Lord of the Rings*—J.R.R. Tolkien
- *Sprightly Running: Part of an Autobiography*—a memoir by John Wain, recounting much of the Inklings' interactions.
- *The War in Heaven*—Charles Williams
- *The Place of the Lion*—Charles Williams
- *Many Dimensions*—Charles Williams
- *The Greater Trumps*—Charles Williams
- *Descent Into Hell*—Charles Williams
- *All Hallows' Eve*—Charles Williams
- *A Study of Old English Literature*—C.L. Wrenn

Appendix B: A Brief Inklings Chronology[26]

- May 11, 1926—Lewis and Tolkien first meet at tea for Oxford professors.
- Late fall of 1929, Tolkien gives "The Lay of Leithian" to Lewis to read. Lewis reads it the night of December 6.
- May of 1930—Warren Lewis begins arranging and editing the Lewis family papers.
- September 19–20, 1931—Tolkien, Hugo Dyson, and Lewis have a nighttime conversation along Addison's Walk. Lewis learns that Christianity has all the elements of a great myth, but with the one exception, that it really happened. Christianity is true and meaningful, for the intellect and imagination.
- September 28, 1931—While riding in his brother's side-car to the Whipsnade Zoo, Lewis becomes a Christian.
- Late 1932—Lewis reads a draft of *The Hobbit*.

- December 21, 1932—Warren moves into The Kilns, Lewis's Oxford home.
- Fall Term of 1933—The Inklings assemble for the first time.
- March 11, 1936—Charles Williams receives a letter from C.S. Lewis, in appreciation for his novel *The Place of the Lion* and invites him to join the Inklings some time.
- Spring of 1936—Lewis and Tolkien discuss a collaborative work; Lewis will write on space travel, while Tolkien will write on time travel.
- December 1937—Tolkien begins writing *The Lord of the Rings.*
- March 4, 1938—Tolkien shares early chapters of *The Lord of the Rings* to Lewis and his son, Christopher; it was enthusiastically received.
- March 8, 1939—Tolkien delivers his essay "On Fairy Stories" at the University of St. Andrews, Scotland.
- September 7, 1939—C. Williams moves from London to Oxford in his post at Oxford University Press.
- October 14, 1940—*The Problem of Pain* is published, dedicated to the Inklings.
- 1942—Lewis publishes *The Screwtape Letters*, dedicated to Tolkien.
- 1942—Williams publishes *The Forgiveness of Sins*, dedicated to the Inklings.
- May 15, 1945—the sudden death of Charles Williams.
- October 20, 1949—The last Inklings meeting in Lewis's rooms on a Thursday evening recorded in W.H. Lewis's diary. The individuals and group continued to meet informally until Lewis's death in 1963.

Appendix C: A Few Good Books About the Inklings

- *The Inklings: C.S. Lewis, J.R.R. Tolkien, Charles Williams and Their Friends* by Humphrey Carpenter
- *J.R.R. Tolkien: A Biography* by Humphrey Carpenter
- *Tolkien and C.S. Lewis: The Gift of Friendship* by Colin Duriez
- *The Oxford Inklings: Their Lives, Writings, Ideas, and Influence* by Colin Duriez

- *Bandersnatch: C.S. Lewis, J.R.R. Tolkien, and the Creative Collaboration of the Inklings* by Diana Pavlac Glyer
- *The Company They Keep: C.S. Lewis, J.R.R. Tolkien as Writers in Community* by Diana Pavlac Glyer
- *From Atheism to Christianity: The Story of C.S. Lewis* by Joel D. Heck
- *A Hobbit, A Wardrobe, and a Great War* by Joseph Loconte
- *On the Shoulders of Hobbits: The Road to Virtue with Tolkien and Lewis* by Louis Markos
- *C.S. Lewis: A Life: Eccentric Genius, Reluctant Prophet* by Alister McGrath
- *The Fellowship: The Literary Lives of the Inklings: J.R.R. Tolkien, C.S. Lewis, Owen Barfield, Charles Williams* by Philip Zaleski and Carol Zaleski

Friendship and the Apologetics of Imagination

Middle-earth and Narnia

Samuel P. Schuldheisz, MDiv

Friendship exhibits a glorious "nearness by resemblance" to Heaven itself where the very multitude of the blessed (which no man can number) increases the fruition which each has for God.[1]

To the Ancients, Friendship seemed the happiest and most fully human of all loves; the crown of life and the school of virtue. The modern world, in comparison, ignores it.[2]

—C.S. Lewis

C.S. Lewis's words about friendship could just as easily have been written today. Social media promises us the ability to interact with friends near and far as well as with billions of people worldwide. Yet, many people are starved for true friendship. Friendship has been reduced to the number of followers, friend requests, and "likes" we have. In the digital age, a good friend is really hard to find.

God's gift of friendship, like that of C.S. Lewis and J.R.R. Tolkien, gives us hope. Together, they sought to reclaim friendship in their daily and literary lives. They did this the best way they knew how. They gathered in Lewis's rooms at Magdalen College to read aloud and critique works in progress with like-minded friends. They strolled along Addison's walk in Oxford, engaging in thoughtful conversation. Encouraged and emboldened by their friendship, Lewis and Tolkien created two of the greatest works of literature, fantasy, and the imagination in all of literature.

In many ways, opening the pages of Tolkien's *The Hobbit* or *The Lord of the Rings* or Lewis's *Chronicles of Narnia* is like visiting with a good friend. No matter how many times you meet there is always something new to discover. Whether you have known them for a short time or a long while, you feel as if you have known them for a lifetime. Then, before you know it, the hours have passed you by, and upon parting you instantly long for your next visit.

Without friendship, we might make it through life, but the journey would be more impoverished, arduous, and lonely. With a good friend at our side, there is joy, companionship, and countless blessings along the way.

From the trenches in the Great War to their booth at the Eagle and the Child, Lewis and Tolkien survived and thrived because of their close friendships. They saw friendship as a gift of God to be received, enjoyed, and shared. Louis Markos observes, "Lewis and Tolkien viewed friendship as an almost spiritual thing, something that transcended the physical without abandoning it."[3] Friendship is a glimpse of eternal joy here on earth and a love that reflects God's love for us in Christ. The friendships within their worlds of Narnia and Middle-earth reveal this as well.

Faith, Hope, and Love

In his chapter on friendship in *The Four Loves*, Lewis writes that "friendship can be a school of virtue."[4] Who better to teach us about friendship and virtue than two of the greatest professors and friends of the twentieth century: C.S. Lewis and J.R.R. Tolkien? Friendship surrounds virtually every character, story, and adventure in their imaginative worlds of Middle-earth and Narnia. Though faith, hope, and love are often known as the theological virtues, they are also virtues found within the friendships of these worlds.

A good friend, after all, is trustworthy, dependable, and faithful. And there is no one more faithful in Middle-earth than Tolkien's beloved creatures, the hobbits. Chief among the hobbits is Samwise Gamgee. Toward the beginning of *The Lord of the Rings*, Frodo plans to leave the Shire for the elven home of Rivendell, taking the One Ring with him. But he wouldn't get far without his good and faithful friend Samwise.

> "If you don't come back, sir, then I shan't, that's certain," said Sam. *"Don't you leave him!* they said to me. *Leave him!* I said. *I never mean to. I am going with him, if he climbs to the Moon, and if any of those Black Riders try to stop him, they'll have Sam Gamgee to reckon with."*[5]

Such is the nature of a good friend, faithful even unto death.

Despite countless dangers, and against overwhelming odds, Samwise was determined to follow Frodo to their journey's end. As their journey progresses, however, Frodo fears he cannot even trust his faithful friend. Two of Frodo's other close friends, Meriadoc Brandybuck and Peregrin Took (affectionately known as Merry and Pippin), discover his secret plans to leave the Shire for Rivendell. Merry and Pippin quickly dispel Frodo's fears, however.

> "It all depends on what you want," put in Merry. "You can trust us to stick to you through thick and thin—to the bitter end. And you can trust us to keep any secret of yours—closer than you keep it yourself. But you cannot trust us to let you face trouble alone, and go off without a word. We are your friends, Frodo. Anyway, there it is. We know most of what Gandalf has told you. We know a good deal about the Ring. We are horribly afraid—but we are going with you, or following you like hounds."[6]

Merry and Pippin are true to their word, as is Samwise, following Frodo from the Shire to Rivendell and beyond, all under the watchful eye of Sauron's restless evil.

Later, when Frodo chooses the heavy burden of being the ring bearer at the Council of Elrond, Samwise chimes in without hesitation.

> "But you won't send him off alone surely, Master?" cried Sam, unable to contain himself any longer, and jumping up from the corner where he had been quietly sitting on the floor.
> "No indeed!" said Elrond, turning towards him with a smile. "You at least shall go with him. It is hardly possible to separate you from him, even when he is summoned to a secret meeting and you are not."[7]

Samwise further reveals his loyalty and fidelity when the Fellowship breaks apart at Amon Hen. Without hesitation, he flings himself like a lemming into the river to follow Frodo on to Mordor. Frodo protests his coming; the road ahead is fraught with danger. But Samwise insists. The faithfulness of friendship prevails. "I know that well enough, Mr. Frodo. Of course you are. And I'm coming with you . . . I'm coming too, or neither of us isn't going. I'll knock holes in all the boats first."[8] Though Sam has no way of knowing the perils ahead of them, he knows that leaving his friend alone would be far worse. Sam will not be "the faithless one, who says farewell when the road darkens."[9]

Again and again Samwise proves to be one of the greatest Christ-figures in *The Lord of the Rings*. In his faithfulness, love, and friendship with Frodo, he demonstrates the humility and love of Christ for us. Just as Samwise carried Frodo and the burden of the One Ring up the slopes of Mt. Doom, Jesus carries the great burden of our sin up the slopes of Mt. Calvary. "'Come, Mr. Frodo!' he cried. 'I can't carry it for you, but I can carry you and it as well. So up you get! Come on, Mr. Frodo dear! Sam will give you a ride. Just tell him where to go, and he'll go.'"[10]

In the closing chapters of *The Lord of the Rings*, Frodo and Samwise appear to be at the end of their journey as well. Hope for rescue looked bleak. Nevertheless, Frodo says to his friend: "The Quest is achieved, and now all is over. I am glad you are here with me. Here at the end of all things, Sam."[11]

Friendship also abounds in Narnia. From the first time we enter through the wardrobe with Lucy, Lewis writes in his fictional characters many of the qualities of friendship he shared with his friends. Lucy and Tumnus the fawn quickly become friends over tea and conversation. Mr. and Mrs. Beaver befriend the four Pevensies, providing them food, shelter, and safe passage to Aslan. The peculiar marshwiggle, Puddleglum, accompanies Jill and Eustace along their perilous journey to rescue Prince Rillian.

Lewis also paints a sublime portrait of hope in his character Reepicheep, the noble talking mouse we first meet in *Prince Caspian*. As *The Voyage of the Dawn Treader* begins, Reepicheep inspires his friends with his hope that their journey to find the seven lost lords of Narnia would lead them to a higher hope on a greater shore. "As high as my spirit," it said. 'Though perhaps as small as my stature. Why should we not come to the very eastern end of the world? And what might we find there? I expect to find Aslan's own country. It is always from the east, across the sea, that the great Lion comes to us.'"[12]

Reepicheep's hope is infectious, filling Edmund and Lucy with awe and wonder. They had seen Aslan before in their previous adventures in Narnia. They longed to see him again, especially Lucy. If anyone dared to call Aslan their friend, it was Lucy.

To be sure, Aslan is not a tame lion, but he is good. More than that, Aslan is the Christ-figure in Narnia. He trades places with Edmund to save him and all Narnia from the White Witch's curse. Like good friends, Lucy and her sister, Susan, followed Aslan to the stone table where he was sacrificed. After waiting and watching throughout the night, they were the first to see him alive again the next morning. Lucy and Aslan romped with joy. Lucy received the high honor of riding atop Aslan's back, to touch his mane, and walk with him in counsel. When Lucy and Edmund departed Narnia for their own world in the final time in *Dawn Treader*, Aslan reassures them. "There I have another name. You must learn to know me by that name. This was the very reason why you were brought to Narnia, that by knowing me here for a little, you may know me better there."[13]

At other times in these two great stories, trust must be built, proven, and restored. Middle-earth and Narnia are also home to stories of reconciliation between friends and enemies. Aslan restores and reconciles Edmund with his siblings after the stone table is cracked. Eustace gradually becomes a good friend to Lucy and Edmund after he becomes un-dragoned by Aslan on Dragon Island.

An extraordinary transformation, from enemies to friends, occurs in the unlikely friendship of Gimli and Legolas. Their friendship is further evidence that Lewis was right in calling friendship a type of love. "Indeed," writes Louis Markos, "of all the friendships in *The Lord of the Rings*, the most remarkable is the one that slowly develops between Gimli the Dwarf and Legolas the Elf. Though their races have been bitter enemies for many generations, the stubborn, feisty Dwarf and the aloof, distant Elf form a bond that promises a healing and reconciliation that no victory on the battlefield could ever accomplish."[14]

During the battle of Helm's Deep, the strength and beauty of their friendship is revealed. Gimli and Legolas make a promise to one another, to visit the forests of Fangorn and the caverns within the fortress of Helms Deep once there is peace. Their promise reveals their mutual love, humility, and friendship.

> Almost you make me regret that I have not seen these caves. Come! Let us make this bargain—if we both return safe out of the peril that awaits us, we will journey for a while together. You shall visit Fangorn with me, and then I will come with you to see Helm's Deep.[15]

The friendship we see between Legolas and Gimli is repeated throughout Middle-earth and Narnia. The faith, hope, and love shared between friends bears the fruit of humility and sacrifice.

Humility and Sacrifice

C.S. Lewis learned many things from reading G.K. Chesterton, and chief among them was the art of observing and upholding paradoxes in the Christian life. In *Mere Christianity*, Lewis observes one of these great paradoxes. Those who are humble insist they are not, while those who are prideful also insist they are not. Ironically, writes Lewis, the one who is humble "will not be thinking about humility: he will not be thinking about himself at all."[16]

Lewis's words on friendship and humility echo St. Paul's words about humility and Christ's sacrifice in Philippians 2:4–8.

> Let each of you look not only to his own interests, but also to the interests of others. Have this mind among yourselves, which is yours in Christ Jesus, who, though he was in the form of God, did not count equality with God a thing to be grasped, but emptied himself, by taking the form of a servant, being born in the likeness of men. And being found in human form, he humbled himself by becoming obedient to the point of death, even death on a cross.

Humility and sacrifice are the center of Christianity, though it is not the individual Christian's humility and sacrifice that take center stage. After all, Paul does not teach that we are saved by Christ being an example of humility and sacrifice. Rather, we are saved by Christ's humility and sacrifice on our behalf. By grace you are saved. We love because Christ first loved us.

Humility and sacrifice are also the center of many stories and characters in Narnia and Middle-earth. Through their stories, Lewis and Tolkien give us a glimpse of the one true story of humility and sacrifice in Christ's death on the cross.

Humility and sacrifice are where the great love of friendship is revealed. Caspian yields his desire to see Aslan's country for the sake of his friends, crew, and kingdom at the end of *The Voyage of the Dawn Treader*. Gandalf throws himself down into the deep to save the Fellowship from the Balrog in Moria. Aragorn, Gimli, and Legolas chase down Saruman's wicked Uruk-Hai to rescue Merry and Pippin. Aslan gave himself up to the White Witch, her stone knife, and the stone table. Her victory, however, was short lived, as Aslan declares.

> For there is a magic deeper still which she did not know. Her knowledge goes back only to the dawn of time. But if she could have looked back a little further, into the stillness and the darkness before Time dawned, she would have read there a different incantation. She would have known that when a willing victim who had committed no treachery was killed in the traitor's stead, the Table would crack and Death itself would start working backward.[17]

Friendship, writes Lewis, "Is the most spiritual of loves . . . It is the sort of love one can imagine between angels."[18] For Lewis and Tolkien, the gift of friendship was both transcendent and spiritual (a gift of God whereby we glimpse the divine), but also imminent and earthly, affecting our daily lives. In Tolkien's *The Hobbit*, Thorin Oakenshield is changed because of his friendship with Bilbo Baggins. Shortly before his death after the Battle of Five Armies, Thorin Oakenshield, leader of the company of dwarves, thanks Bilbo for his humility, sacrifice, and friendship. "If more of us valued food and cheer and song above hoarded gold, it would be a merrier world. But sad or merry, I must leave it now. Farewell!"[19]

Conclusion

Sacrifice and humility lead to joy in friendship. At the end of *The Hobbit*, Bilbo welcomes the company of dwarves he had traveled with to visit his home at Bag End as often as they like. At the end of *The Lord of the Rings*, Frodo and Bilbo depart Middle-earth for the joys of the undying lands in the West. At the end of *The Last Battle*, Lewis tells us that the children regularly gather together to talk of the serious business of Narnia.

This is what friends do. They laugh, eat, drink, talk, read, write, think, and enjoy each other's company. They share the trials, pain, and suffering of life. Most of all, they share the joy and love of friendship.

Tolkien and Lewis shared many things in their friendship. Most important of all was their faith in Christ. Through his friend Tolkien, Lewis was brought back to the Christian faith. Tolkien taught Lewis that Christianity is the greatest story of all because it is the one myth (that is, story) that actually happened. Because of his friendship with Tolkien and the other Inklings, Lewis was inspired to write some of the greatest Christian books of the twentieth century. Lewis, in turn, was a source of encouragement, appreciation, and companionship to his friend, Tolkien.

It was storytelling that first brought Lewis and Tolkien together as friends when they discovered their mutual love of Norse mythology. Their friendship, along with the friendships found within their writings, continue to inspire readers and writers alike. Good stories have a way of bringing people together, as they did for Tolkien and Lewis. In friendship, Christ's love and his saving Gospel are given and proclaimed to others. "Friendship," writes Lewis, "is the instrument by which God reveals to each the beauties of all the others."[20]

In the real-world friendship of Lewis and Tolkien, and through friendships in their literary worlds, we also see an apologetic for the Christian faith. Through storytelling, myth, and the Gospel, Tolkien gave his friend Lewis a reason for the hope that was within him.

Tolkien and Lewis never set out on a missionary journey like that of St. Paul, nor did they intend to. Still, their books, ideas, and faith have spread around the world, carrying the joy of good stories, the love of friendship, and the good news of the Gospel with them. Lewis and Tolkien were apostles of the imagination and the intellect. In their vocation as writers, they declared and defended the Gospel through their storytelling and scholarship alike.

In our friendships we can do the same, in whatever it is we have in common with our friends. In love of friendship, we share the love of Christ with others. In God's gift of friendship, we see the love of his Son, Christ our Lord, the friend of sinners.

In the kindness of a good friend, we see Christ's kindness. His love for us is patient and kind beyond measure. In the humility of a good friend, we see Christ's humility. For the joy set before him, Christ endured the cross for us. In the love of a good friend, we see Christ's love. While we were still sinners, Christ died for us.

Friendship in Middle-earth and Narnia is no different. In the faithfulness, loyalty, and sacrifice of Samwise, we see a picture of our Lord who was faithful unto death for us. In the reconciliation and friendship between Gimli and Legolas, we see our Lord, who has reconciled all things to himself in the cross. In Reepicheep's infectious joy, we glimpse the eternal joy of our own true country where Christ, the Lion of Judah and Lamb of God, is our light and life. In Aslan's love for Edmund, Lucy, Susan, and Peter, we see Christ's love for us.

In the Gospel we hear the true story of Jesus, who is the friend of sinners, who laid down his life for us. May the friendship of Lewis and Tolkien, and the friendships within the pages of their literary worlds, enrich our friendships in this world and, above all, point us to the greatest friendship of all.

> Greater love has no one than this, that someone lay down his life for his friends. (John 15:13)

Friendship in the Lutheran Confessions

The Mutual Consolation of the Brethren

David J. Rufner, MDiv

In the last chapter of a book devoted to friendship, what more can be said? In particular, what can be said about friendship from the Lutheran Confessions?

After mining the scriptures, surveying some of the best of historic Western thought, and sitting at the feet of the master C.S. Lewis, is there really any hope of finding anything in the Lutheran Confessions that will also sing to the hungry heart of friendship? Or do we have here a closing consideration with no punch at all?

In the beginning of the Gospel of John, Nathaniel challenged Philip, "Can anything good come from Nazareth?" The reader of course knows that the answer is *yes*, for Jesus himself comes from Nazareth. Still, Philip's reply is telling and informative. He simply said, "Come, let us see!" (John 1:43–46).

We might ask a similar question: "The Confessions? Can anything good on the topic of friendship come from the Lutheran Confessions?" The answer I propose is a hearty yes. And here, also, the hearty yes is anchored on the person and work of Jesus Christ. Therefore, come and let us see!

Survey

Any cursory search of *The Book of Concord* would lead a seeker to initial hopefulness. *Friend* and its cognates appear nearly fifty times.:

> Gracious allies are *friends* (32:12, 33:10, 35:17).
>
> In a discussion over whether the will is free or bound, it is insisted that the will is powerless to choose "the righteousness of God or spiritual [things]" (51:1–2), yet we have some freedom for producing civil righteousness and for choosing things subject to reason, such as "whether to work in the field or not, whether to eat and drink, [and] whether to visit a *friend* or not" (52:5).
>
> Christ as propitiator is likened to "when a person pays a debt for *friends,* [and] the debtors are freed by the merit of the other" (240:19).
>
> In a discussion on monastic vows, there is mention of those "whom parents and *friends* pushed into the monasteries" under duress (278:9). And, "In the same way, it is silly to maintain that it is an act of devotion to God to leave possessions, *friends*, wife, and children without the command of God" (284:42).

A reader will find that a majority of the references to *friends* and *friendship* are taken up in a variety of conversations, each weighty, each consequential, yet each somewhat unique. Together, they don't comprise a singular vision of friendship, or what we might call a theology of friendship in the Lutheran Confessions. Still, all is not lost, for while a majority of the references don't prove helpful to our search, there is still a word on friendship in the Confessions.

This voice is clear. This voice is helpful. This voice is compelling. And this voice is the voice of none other than Martin Luther himself in both the Small and Large Catechisms, with a few glorious sentences about the Gospel of Jesus Christ tucked inside the Smalcald Articles. It is to this voice and these writings that we now direct our attention.

Friendship in Luther's Small and Large Catechism

While Luther, Melanchthon, and the other Reformers desired a full church council for Christendom in which to make their case before both pope and emperor, this hardly slowed them from the pastoral care of the people. Formulas, apologies, and treatises were formulated and are still studied and normative today. Though it is refreshing to both argue and consider that the height of Lutheran theology came when Luther followed the Gospel of Jesus Christ on its holy pilgrimage, Luther was the clearest when he was back home on the ground level and with ordinary people: husband, wife, children, house, home, vocations, neighbors, and authorities.

In fact, this is the very nature of the Small Catechism—the Gospel in and for our daily lives. This is evidenced in its opening words: "As the head of the home should teach them in a simple way to his household." Likewise, in the preface to the Large Catechism, Luther gives admonition to both local pastors and heads of households to be lifelong students of the catechisms and therefore the entire theology of the scriptures. Why so? "So that all who wish to be Christians in fact as well as in name, both young and old may be well trained."[1]

Is it any surprise, then, that at the ground level of the Gospel of Jesus Christ in the midst of day-to-day Christian living we begin to find our theology of friendship in the Lutheran Confessions? It is no real surprise at all.

It is in the first part of the catechism, the Ten Commandments, that all of these ground-level discussions are first taken up. Whereas the first three of commandments take up the question of man's standing before God, beginning at the fourth the discussion of man's standing before his many neighbors is considered.[2] A quick glimpse at the commandments and explanations in the Small Catechism will, in fact, give us nearly everyone already mentioned above—husband and wife, father and mother, children, neighbors, and authorities.

In Luther's explanation of the fourth commandment in the Large Catechism, we finally find the topic of friendship mentioned in a way meaningful for our discussion here. Luther writes:

> Furthermore, in connection with this commandment, we must mention the sort of obedience due to superiors, persons whose duty it is to command and to govern. For all other authority is derived and developed out of the authority of parents. Where a father is unable

by himself to bring up his child, he calls upon a schoolmaster to teach
him; if he is too weak, he seeks the help of his friends and neighbors;
if he dies, he confers and delegates his responsibility and authority to
others appointed for the purpose.[3]

Characteristic of Luther and his instruction on the commandments is how he consistently demonstrates not only what the commandments call for or prohibit but also a broader world of duty and
life to which they point. This fourth commandment, which is given
in the positive—what we are called to do—is similarly expanded by
Luther. He freely names the types of activities that it warns against,
such as activities that "despise or anger" our parents, and he calls us
to positive activities, activities that have both an initial mark and a
broadening horizon. The initial mark here is clearly parents, while
the broadening horizon includes "other authorities."[4]

In this case, as with all of the commandments, the view is
toward duty. The first three commandments instruct me concerning
my duties to God, his name, and the sabbath day that he gives me.
Then, starting at the fourth commandment, I am instructed concerning my duties to my various neighbors, that which husbands
owe to wives, wives to husband, parents to children, children to parents, neighbor to neighbor, and so on.

In light of the fourth commandment, then, we return to the
topic at hand, namely friendship. From this same commandment,
Luther points us to what we owe to those above us (all authorities
in whose care we reside), as well has what we owe to those below
us (those in our care). Luther then names the blessing of friends as
those, among others, who will help us to fulfill our duties to those
in our care when we cannot. In short, friends help us uphold the
demands of the law, particularly the second table of the law, which
speaks clearly of our duties to others.

But is this all we can say about friends and friendship? Are these
simply those who have our back when it comes to the keeping of the
demands of the law in the care of others? To be sure, this is a great
blessing and at times would prove a sure comfort, particularly in the
face of trials such as sickness and especially death. In fact, it may be
this blessed facet of friendship that we see at work when Jesus speaks
from the cross to his own mother and the disciple John:

> When Jesus saw his mother and the disciple whom he loved standing nearby, he said to his mother, "Woman, behold, your son!" Then he said to the disciple, "Behold, your mother!" And from that hour the disciple took her to his own home.[5]

In this way, John is a great gift and friend to Jesus. But again, is this all that can be said of friendship in the Lutheran Confessions? No.

In the Small and Large Catechism, we also see friendship addressed in Luther's exposition of the eighth commandment, concerning false testimony and neighbors. He writes:

> [T]he authorities, fathers and mothers, and even brothers and sisters and other good friends are under a mutual obligation to reprove evil wherever it is necessary and helpful.[6]

The prohibition of the eighth commandment means that "we do not tell lies about our neighbor, betray him, slander him, or hurt his reputation," but rather we are to "defend him, speak well of him, and explain everything in the kindest way."[7] Unlike the fourth commandment, this commandment is stated in the negative. Still, here too Luther finds warning and prescription in relation to the duties owed to the various neighbors that the command has in its sights. Before others we are to speak well of our neighbors, speak truthfully about them, and even defend their good name.

Yet, face-to-face with this neighbor, I am to speak truthfully to them and even "reprove evil" with an eye toward saving them from the folly of their actions or beliefs. Simply put, then, friends are also those who, along with father, mother, brothers, and sisters, love me enough to admonish and reprove me "wherever it is necessary and helpful."

As with the consideration of the fourth commandment above, we see that in this one also our friends serve as functionaries of the law, even if graciously so. They help us fulfill our duties when we cannot. And now, also, we see that they are among those under obligation to admonish us—to place the mirror of the law before our eyes—when we are harming any of our various neighbors by failing in our duties to them.

At this point, it is likely that we can begin to think of specific times when our own friends have acted in these ways toward us. They've loved us enough to speak to us honestly, openly, and even forcefully about our foolishness. And they've either stood in the gap, or there is a deep understanding that they will stand in the gap on the day when sickness or death prevent us from being able to fulfill our loving duties to those in our care. Insofar as we have friends in our lives who act in these ways, we can count ourselves blessed and gifted by God.

In fact, Luther spots this very thing and puts it before our eyes in the third part of both the Small and Large Catechisms when he takes up the Lord's Prayer. In the midst of that prayer, we ask God our Father to "give us this day our daily bread." Luther then continues in the Small Catechism to ask a question about this and give an answer:

> What is meant by daily bread? Daily bread includes everything that has to do with the support and needs of the body, such as food, drink, clothing, shoes, house, home, land, animals, money, goods, a devout husband or wife, devout children, devout workers, devout and faithful rulers, good government, good weather, peace, health, self-control, good reputation, good friends, faithful neighbors, and the like.[8]

Good friends are certainly a portion of the "daily bread" that God our Father gives to us. In particular, they help and assist us in the carrying out of our duties toward our many neighbors. Yet, what about the day in which we aren't simply in need of assistance in carrying out our duties? What about the day in which we have completely failed to carry out our duties? In what ways are our friends a help to us when we've harmed our neighbors, either by our actions or inaction? Admonishment may stop me in my tracks, but it is not strong enough to cover over my guilt and shame. Friends may indeed come to my aid in fulfilling my duties in the event of sickness or death. But these same friends cannot heal or bring life to death.

Their presence and actions in my life are certainly gifts of God. Still, we must admit that the vision of friendship to this point in the confessions is still limited and incapable of accounting for life's most difficult circumstances.

Friendship in Luther's Smalcald Articles

For the reasons named above we can be thankful for a final writing on the topic of friendship from the pen of Luther. This last bit comes to us from the Smalcald Articles, written in 1537. In these articles, Luther sought to summarize what he considered to be the most essential teachings of the Christian faith to comfort those whose "sins burden" them.[9] Here too, Luther follows the pilgrimage of the Gospel as it comes to ordinary people in ordinary circumstances. Of greatest interest to us, then, is Article III.4, "Concerning the Gospel." Luther writes:

> We now want to return to the gospel, which gives guidance and help against sin in more than one way, because God is extravagantly rich in his grace: first, through the spoken word, in which the forgiveness of sins is preached to the whole world (which is the proper function of the gospel); second, through baptism; third, through the holy Sacrament of the Altar; fourth, through the power of the keys and also through the mutual conversation and consolation of brothers and sisters. Matthew 18[:20]: "Where two or three are gathered . . ."[10]

God our father is certainly rich toward us. He gives us daily bread in many forms, including in the form of friends who graciously come to our aid and even admonish and rebuke us when we are in danger of falling, or in fact have fallen, short of fulfilling our duties to our many neighbors. Still, there are momentous times when such daily bread will prove too little. Friends on their own can do nothing about the guilt and shame of my sin. Nor are they able to do anything to change the fact of my death on the day it occurs.

To this severe weakness, to this great limitation, Luther now brings the best of news by way of the Gospel of Jesus Christ in which "God is extravagantly rich in his grace." Luther tells us that this extravagance comes through the Gospel preached and proclaimed, is given again in baptism, and is given yet again in the holy sacrament of the Lord's Supper. But Luther does not stop there precisely because God our Father does not stop here in relation to how rich he is with his Gospel of grace in Jesus Christ. Instead, going further, Luther gives us a fourth "way" of the Gospel: "[The Gospel is also at work] through the power of the keys and also through the mutual conversation and consolation of brothers and sisters."[11]

On the lips of our friends who are themselves gifts of "daily bread," God our Father puts the Gospel of Jesus Christ who is himself the eternal "bread of life" (John 6:48). Or in short, in our friendships daily bread now carries to us the bread of life. Good and great friends deliver to us the promises and gifts of our greater and greatest friend, Christ Jesus (John 15:15).

What gifts are these? These are words of forgiveness and absolution. These are words that cover guilt and take away shame. These are words of God's peace toward those who neither have it in themselves, nor do they deserve it. These are words of promise for new life to come. In short, these are words of comfort for sinners who have themselves sinned and broken much, because first and foremost they are slaves to sin.

But where does one friend—one brother or sister in the faith—get off declaring peace, forgiveness, hope, and a new life? How exactly do they dare to offer such comfort, conversation, and consolation? And even if they are bold enough to speak such words, where exactly does the strength come to make good on these words and promises? After all, we've already outlined the very limits of friendship and how there are gaps too big for us to fill, such as on the occasion of death and in the face of guilt and shame. The answer to all of these questions and the source of this new and "extravagant" dimension to friendships is Jesus Christ and his Gospel. It is the very same Jesus who wiped away all guilt and accusations that stood against you by paying for them with his very life on the cross and by declaring that news to you on the lips of another, who now uses you to declare his forgiveness to me! The very same Jesus who used one of your brothers or sisters in the faith to declare his promise of raising you from the grave to new life now uses you, my friend, to declare the same to me! The very same Jesus who, in his resurrection, came at you, not with anger and revenge, but with his peace, and spoke that peace to you on the lips of another, now uses you, my friend, to speak to me and comfort me with God's peace in Christ Jesus!

The great thing about friends in this life is that you can't shake them off. In times of distress, they are there to fill in where our strength and life have left off. On the day we cause others distress, they are there in our face, bringing sobriety and repentance, lead-ing to a gentle and gracious return. But the best of all friendships are rooted in the Gospel of Jesus Christ, where we declare time and again the faithfulness of God the Father through Jesus Christ, his dear Son, our Lord. In essence, we say this to each other: God the Father has loved you through Jesus Christ, and there is nothing you can do about it. You're just going to have to deal with it. There's no shaking him off!

May you give such consolation to your brothers and sisters in Christ and, in so doing, be a true friend to them. And may you receive it just the same from those whom you are privileged to count as your friends—all on account of Christ Jesus our Lord.

Postscript

In the nearly ten years between when Luther authored the catechisms and the Smalcald Articles, it is no exaggeration to say that Luther experienced a difficult season in life. Among his many trials was his declining health. Beginning in 1531 and ending with his death in 1546, he suffered from fainting, kidney stones, vertigo, tinnitus, a cataract, angina, and multiple heart attacks, including the one that finally took his life.

In fact, because of one of these illnesses, he was not able to attend the Schmalkaldic League meetings in 1537. This alone is of minor historic interest and ultimately of little importance to our consideration of friendship in the Lutheran Confessions. However, one related piece of history will prove of more interest to us.

A note comes down to us about Luther's writing of the Smalcald Articles themselves, in the time leading up to the Schmalkaldic League meetings. After writing about repentance and before address-ing the Gospel and the mutual consolation of the saints, Luther suf-fered a heart attack. From this point forward, Luther was forced to dictate the rest of the Smalcald Articles to Caspar Cruciger Sr. and another unknown secretary.[12]

We see here, in Luther's life, some of the very things he wrote about. In the face of sickness and even the possibility of death, sev-eral came to him and served him as a true brother and themselves as true friends. Where he was unable in his weakness to fulfill one of his duties, they faithfully stepped in and helped.

Were they during this same time declaring to him the very comfort of Jesus, the "mutual conversation and consolation" that friends bring to each other in the face of distress? It seems more than possible and even likely. In fact, it is a sweet thought to consider that the comfort of such consolation from friends, rooted in the Gospel of Jesus Christ, was what led him to include the blessings of the Gospel received from our friends. Yet ultimately, it is also too much to insist that it was so. It cannot be proven.

Still, even if we can't prove it here, we can find such consolation in 1546, in Eisleben, Germany, on Luther's deathbed. There in the early hours of the morning of February 18, Luther recited Psalm 31:5: "Into your hand, I commit my spirit; you have redeemed me, O LORD, faithful God." His friends Michael Coelius and Justus Jonas warmed him with hot towels and spoke the promises of God in Christ to him. Then in loud voices they asked him, "Reverend Father, are you ready to die trusting in your Lord Jesus Christ and to confess the doctrine which you have taught in his name?" And Luther replied, "Yes."[13] He then died shortly after at 2:45 a.m.

And so, for a second time I say: May you give such consolation to your brothers and sisters in Christ and, in doing so, be a true friend to them. And may you receive it just the same from those whom you are privileged to count as your friends—all on account of Christ Jesus our Lord.

Notes

Where Two or Three Are Gathered—An Introduction

¹ For more, see: Diana Pavlac Glyer, *The Company They Keep: C.S. Lewis and J.R.R. Tolkien as Writers in Community* (Kent, OH: Kent State University Press, 2007).

² "2.5 million men 'have no close friends,'" last modified November 14, 2015, https://www.telegraph.co.uk/men/active/mens-health/11996473/2.5-million-men-have-no-close-friends.html.

³ Mark Greene, "Why Do We Murder the Beautiful Friendships of Boys?," Fatherly, last modified September 14, 2017, https://www.fatherly.com/love-money/dangerous-side-effects-discouraging-male-friendship/.

⁴ Each Mind Matters: Mental Health, accessed April 7, 2019, https://promisetotalk.org/documents/Depression_Men_FactSheet.pdf.

⁵ "Suicide Statistics," AFSP, last modified March 12, 2019, https://afsp.org/about-suicide/suicide-statistics/.

⁶ WA 42:501.

⁷ Trgl, *The Smalcald Articles,* Part III, Article IV.

Theology of Friendship

¹ C.S. Lewis, *The Four Loves* (New York: Mariner Books, 2012), 80.

² Marcus Tullius Cicero, "On Friendship," in *The Harvard Classics,* vol. 9, trans. E.S. Shuchburgh (New York: P.F. Collier & Son, 1965), 17.

³ BOC, *The Smalcald Articles,* Part III, Article 4, 319.

Friendship in the Old Testament

¹ Abraham Heschel, *Man is not Alone: A Philosophy of Religion* (Philadelphia: Jewish Publication Society, 1951), 129.

² "In Adam We Have All Been One," *Lutheran Service Book,* 569.

³ AE 2:335.

Friendship in the New Testament

[1] Robert Farrar Capon, *Kingdom, Grace, Judgment: Paradox, Outrage, and Vindication in the Parables of Jesus* (Grand Rapids: William B. Eerdmans Publishing Company, 2002), 300.

The Invisible Bond of Friendship from Gilgamesh to Augustine

[1] *The Epic of Gilgamesh,* trans. N.K. Sandars (New York: Penguin, 1960), tablets 9–10.

[2] Homer, *The Iliad*, trans. Robert Fagles (New York: Penguin, 1998), book 18.

[3] Ibid.

[4] Plato, *The Dialogues of Plato*, trans. B. Jowett (Random House, 1937), 318.

[5] Cicero, *On the Good Life,* trans. Michael Grant (New York: Penguin, 1971), 184.

[6] Augustine, *The Confessions of Saint Augustine,* trans. Rex Warner (New York: Signet, 2009), 73.

[7] Ibid., 75.

The Philosophy of Friendship

[1] C.S. Lewis, *The Four Loves* (New York: HarperCollins, 2017), 90.

[2] "Wittgenstein: A Wonderful Life," *Philosophy Now | a Magazine of Ideas*, https://philosophynow.org/issues/58/Wittgenstein_A_Wonderful_Life, accessed April 6, 2019.

[3] Plato, *Complete Works* (Indianapolis: Hackett Publishing, 1997), 704.

[4] Aristotle, *The Basic Works of Aristotle* (New York: Modern Library, 2009), 943.

[5] Augustine, *The Confessions, trans.* Maria Boulding (Hyde Park, NY: New City Press, 1997), 143.

[6] Todd W. Nichol and Marc Kolden, *Called and Ordained: Lutheran Perspectives on the Office of the Ministry* (Eugene: Wipf and Stock Publishers, 2004), 49–55.

The Ethics of Friendship

[1] See Kazoh Kitamori's *Theology of the Pain of God* (Wipf & Stock, 2015) for a robust discussion of this theme. He argues that, unlike Buddhism, which seeks to avoid pain by eliminating desire, Christianity involves a righteous *desire* and care for others, which leads to pain when the beloved is disconnected from the Gospel.

² In my book *Sexy: The Quest for Erotic Virtue in Perplexing Times* (ViW Books, 2017), 135–36, I suggest, somewhat provocatively, that a young person might appropriately say "I love you" on the first date. This is because it is important for folks not to assume that sexualizing a relationship represents some confirmation that love is present in a relationship. Love is the basis of a relationship, understood in Christian terms. A couple continues to date, in view of marriage, not to see whether a romantic partner is worthy of love, but rather whether the couple is able to exist together in a mutual pursuit of goodness, truth, and beauty. Perhaps something like a rich friendship can develop between a husband and wife. But note that liking someone, in this context, is a relatively pragmatic question. So is friendship in general, as I will argue here.

³ Unless otherwise stated, all biblical citations in this chapter are from the English Standard Version.

⁴ Augustine, "Sermon 385," in *The Works of Saint Augustine: A Translation for the Twenty-first Century*, trans. Edmund Hill, ed. John Rotelle (New City Press, 1995), 10: 387.

⁵ For Christian virtue ethics, consider Gilbert Meilaender, *Faith and Faithfulness: Basic Themes in Christian Ethics* (South Bend: Notre Dame, 1993). For historical considerations related to the place of virtue theory within the Lutheran tradition, one might consult Joel Biermann, *A Case for Character: Towards a Lutheran Virtue Ethics* (Fortress, 2014), though I am uneasy with some of the ways in which Biermann applies virtue theory within the context of the Christian church. I outline a better way for understanding virtue in the context of congregational life in my essay: "Virtue Ethics and its Application within Lutheran Congregations," *Issues in Christian Education*, 50.3 (2017), https://issues.cune.edu/educating-in-lutheran-ethics/virtue-ethics-and-its-application-within-lutheran-congregations/.

⁶ Mark Mattes, "Discipleship in Lutheran Perspective," *Lutheran Quarterly* 26 (2012): 150.

⁷ I've had many friendly but intense conversations with fellow Lutherans about whether Lutherans should talk about virtue or emphasize it as a framework for ethics. I think this is because they a) are rightly skeptical about the applicability of Aristotle's approach and b) they probably recall Luther said some very negative things about Aristotle's ethics. If we don't absolutely equate virtue theory with Aristotelian ethics but instead focus on Lutheran virtue ethics flowing from Luther's *The Freedom of a Christian* and perhaps a bit from a source that inspired Luther's thinking, the anonymous *Theologia Germanica*, my approach should be clearer and provide rich, consistent ways of thinking about ethics from a Lutheran perspective. Once this is established, we can "spoil the Egyptians," as it were, and draw from Aristotle's ideas when helpful, leaving them when they don't apply.

⁸ J.K.A. Smith, *Desiring the Kingdom* (Grand Rapids: Baker Academic, 2009).

⁹ To see how dangerous and pervasive this is in society, see Philip Zimbardo, *The Lucifer Effect: Understanding How Good People Turn Evil* (New York: Random House, 2008).

¹⁰ Aristotle, *Nicomachean Ethics,* 1155a.

¹¹ Mary Sim, *Remastering Morals with Aristotle and Confucius* (New York: Cambridge University Press, 2007), 194.

¹² *The Spiritual World of Isaac the Syrian,* Cistercian Studies 175 (Kalamazoo: Cistercian Publications, 2000).

¹³ Dietrich Bonhoeffer, *Ethics* (New York: Touchstone, 1995), 126.

¹⁴ Yim, *Remastering Morals,* 197.

¹⁵ Augustine, "Sermon 336.2," *The Works of Saint Augustine,* 267.

¹⁶ Tamer Nawar, "Augustine on the Dangers of Friendship," *The Classical Quarterly* 65.2 (2015): 836–51.

¹⁷ Incidentally, I find the idea that men and women cannot be friends, and in fact that this is always inappropriate, to be a bit creepy. Granted, it's possible that a particular individual is not self-controlled enough to have friends of the opposite sex without sexualizing the relationship. In such cases, they should of course avoid this. But sometimes I worry that this sort of thinking reveals a fundamentally immature character. In other words, I sometimes worry that a personal rule against a man having a female friend reveals the unfortunate fact that this particular individual primarily views women as potential sexual partners, not human beings with their own autonomy.

¹⁸ C.S. Lewis, preface to *On the Incarnation: Saint Athanasius* (St. Vladimir's Seminary Press, 2012).

¹⁹ See *The Scapegoat* (Baltimore: Johns Hopkins University Press, 1989), *Violence and the Sacred* (New York: Norton, 1979), and *I See Satan Fall Like Lightning* (Ossining, NY: Orbis, 2001).

²⁰ Consider Walter Wink, *Engaging the Powers: Discernment and Resistance in a World of Domination* (Fortress, 1995) for a different take on Girard's idea of the myth of primal violence.

²¹ I don't want to be insensitive here. I'm trying to accurately reflect the sort of thing I've heard in university cafeterias during my nearly two decades of teaching. As a fun side note on how this works, check out Amy Frykholm Johnson's *Rapture Culture: Left Behind in Evangelical America* (2007). She shows how, in the *Left Behind* series, most of the good-looking women are too distracting for the strong evangelical-heterosexual response of the protagonists. So, they end up getting violently killed throughout the series, arguably as a way to remove the sexual tension.

²² If this illustration didn't make sense to you, try this: ever notice that when you are admiring an item—a solitary item—at a store, people around you sometimes start to get extraordinarily interested in that item? That's mimetic desire at work.

[23] Girard, *I See Satan Fall Like Lightning*, 7–9.

[24] My translation of Augustine, *City of God*, 19.8.

Luther and Melanchthon

[1] Philip Schaff, *History of the Christian Church* (Grand Rapids, MI: Eerdmans, 1979), 7: 193.

[2] Robert Kolb, *Bound Choice, Election, and Wittenberg Theological Method: From Martin Luther to the Formula of Concord* (Grand Rapids: Wm. B. Eerdmans Publishing, 2005), 280.

[3] Roland H. Bainton, *Here I Stand: A Life of Martin Luther* (Peabody, MA: Hendrickson, 1950), 92.

[4] CR: 3:827.

[5] Schaff, *History of the Christian Church*, 7:192.

[6] Vilmos Vajta, *Luther and Melanchthon in the History and Theology of the Reformation* (Philadelphia: Muhlenberg Press, 1961), 23.

[7] Martin Luther and Theodore G. Tappert, *Luther: Letters of Spiritual Counsel* (Vancouver: Regent College Publishing, 2003), 146.

[8] Quoted in Anja-Leena Laitakari-Pyykkö, "Philip Melanchthon's Influence on English Theological Thought During the Early English Reformation," Dissertation, University of Helsinki, 2013, 62.

[9] Ibid.

[10] Martin Brecht, *Martin Luther: The Preservation of the Church, 1532–1546* (Minneapolis: Augsburg Fortress, 1987), 210.

[11] Ibid.

[12] Vilmos, *Luther and Melanchthon*, 24.

[13] WATR V, no. 5511 and WA XXX/2 68:8.

[14] See Derek Vissen, *Niels menselijks is mij vreemd: leven en werk Philipus Melanchthon* (Kampen: de Groot Goudrian, 1995), 38.

[15] In 1522 Luther got his hands on a copy of Melanchthon's lectures on Romans and Corinthians and had them published in a combined edition under the titles of *Annotationes Phil. Melanchthonis in Epistolae Pauli ad Romanos et as Corinthios*.

[16] WA 2:443–618.

[17] See Heinz Scheible, "Luther and Melanchthon," *Lutheran Quarterly* 4 (1990): 317–39.

The Inklings

[1] Humphrey Carpenter, *The Inklings: C.S. Lewis, J.R.R. Tolkien, Charles Williams and Their Friends* (London: Harper Collins, 2006), 176.

[2] The other members of the Inklings were J.A.W. Bennett, Lord David Cecil, James Dundas-Grant, Colin Hardie, Robert E. Havard, Gervase Mathew, R.B. McCallum, C.E. Stevens, Christopher Tolkien, John Wain, and C.L. Wrenn.

[3] J.R.R. Tolkien, *The Letters of J.R.R. Tolkien*, ed. Humphrey Carpenter (New York: Houghton Mifflin, 2014), 388.

[4] Clyde S. Kilby, *Tolkien and the Silmarillion: A Glimpse at the Man and His World of Myth* (Wheaton: Harold Shaw Publishers, 1976), 68.

[5] Diana Pavlac Glyer, *Bandersnatch: C.S. Lewis, J.R.R. Tolkien, and the Creative Collaboration of the Inklings* (Kent: Black Squirrel Books, 2016), 29.

[6] Alister McGrath, *C.S. Lewis—A Life: Eccentric Genius, Reluctant Prophet* (Carol Stream: Tyndale House Publishers, 2013),177.

[7] Colin Duriez, *C.S. Lewis: A Biography of Friendship* (Oxford: Lion Hudson, 2013), 140.

[8] C.S. Lewis, *The Four Loves* (New York: Harcourt Books, 1960), 67.

[9] Ibid., 65.

[10] C.S. Lewis, *All My Road Before Me: The Diary of C.S. Lewis, 1922–1927*, ed. Walter Hooper (London: Harcourt Brace Jovanovich, 1991), 393.

[11] Lewis, *The Four Loves*. New, 65.

[12] Ibid., 61.

[13] Tolkien, *The Letters of J.R.R. Tolkien*, ed. Humphrey Carpenter (New York: Houghton Mifflin, 2014), 362.

[14] Alister McGrath, *Eccentric Genius*, 176.

[15] Tolkien, *The Letters of J.R.R. Tolkien*, 388.

[16] Lewis quoted it Colin Duriez, *Lewis and J.R.R. Tolkien: The Gift of Friendship* (Mahwah: Hidden Spring, 2003), 127.

[17] Warren H. Lewis, *Memoirs of the Lewis Family, 1850–1930* (1933), 34.

[18] Diana Pavlac Glyer, *The Company They Keep: C.S. Lewis and J.R.R. Tolkien as Writers in Community* (Kent, OH: Kent State University Press, 2007), 31, 33.

[19] Ibid., 40.

[20] Humphrey Carpenter, *Tolkien: A Biography* (Boston: Houghton Mifflin, 1977), 194.

[21] Alister McGrath, *Eccentric Genius*, 151.

[22] Letter is dated October 18, 1931. Lewis, *The Collected Letters of C.S. Lewis*, ed. Walter Hooper (New York: Harper San Francisco, 2004), 1:977.

[23] Lewis, *The Collected Letters of C.S. Lewis* (New York: Harper San Francisco, 2004), 2:501.

[24] Lewis, *The Four Loves* (New York: Harcourt Books, 1960), 72.

[25] Tolkien, *On Fairy Stories* in *Essays Presented to Charles Williams*, ed. C.S. Lewis (Grand Rapids: Eerdmans Publishing Company, 1968), 83–84.

[26] This chronology is compiled from Colin Duriez's book *Tolkien and C.S. Lewis: The Gift of Friendship*, Alister McGrath's *C.S. Lewis: A Life*, and Diana Pavlac Glyer's book *The Company They Keep*.

Friendship and the Apologetics of Imagination

[1] Lewis, *The Four Loves*, 62.

[2] Ibid., 57.

[3] Louis Markos, *On the Shoulders of Hobbits: The Road to Virtue with Tolkien and Lewis* (Chicago: Moody Publishers, 2012), 106.

[4] Lewis, *The Four Loves*, 80

[5] John R. Tolkien, *The Fellowship of the Ring: The Lord of the Rings—Part One* (New York: Del Rey, 1994), 94.

[6] Ibid.

[7] Ibid., 264.

[8] Ibid., 397.

[9] Ibid.

[10] *The Return of the King*, 940.

[11] Ibid.

[12] *Dawn Treader*, 21.

[13] Ibid., 247.

[14] Louis Markos, *On the Shoulders of Hobbits: The Road to Virtue with Tolkien and Lewis* (Chicago: Moody Publishers, 2012), 111.

[15] *The Two Towers*, 535.

[16] C.S. Lewis, *Mere Christianity* (New York: Macmillian, 1956), 128.

[17] *The Lion, the Witch, and the Wardrobe*, 163.

[18] Ibid., 77, 87.

[19] J.R.R. Tolkien, *The Hobbit: 75th Anniversary Edition* (Boston: Houghton Mifflin Harcourt, 2012), 494.

[20] Ibid., 89.

Friendship in the Lutheran Confessions

[1] BOC, 383.6.

[2] For a masterful, approachable, and devotional discussion of how the second table of the law relates to the first, see James Nestingen and Gerhard O. Forde, *Free to Be* (Minneapolis, MN: Augsburg Fortress, 1993).

[3] BOC, 405:141.

[4] SC, 12.

[5] John 19:26–27 (ESV).

[6] BOC, 422.274.

[7] SC, 13.
[8] SC, 20–21.
[9] BOC, 300.14.
[10] BOC, 319.45.
[11] BOC, 319.
[12] BOC, 127.
[13] Michael Reeves, *The Unquenchable Flame* (Downers Grove: IVP, 2009), 60.

CPSIA information can be obtained
at www.ICGtesting.com
Printed in the USA
LVHW092319071019
633522LV00006B/198/P